'A really helpful, p̲... that is a must read for all leaders within churches. This will actually make your life easier and empower all of your congregations to be effective Christian witnesses everywhere they find themselves.'
Gavin Calver, CEO, Evangelical Alliance

'Jesus commands us to go and make disciples – most of us are well aware of that! But what does disciplemaking actually look like in practice? *Vital Signs* is an engaging, accessible and really practical way to explore this and embed whole-life discipleship more deeply, both personally and among our churches. Ken's clear approach and relevant stories will make this a must read for many. I also loved the prayers at the end of each chapter. They helped me to not just read the words but encouraged me to pause and root these ideas in my spirituality and practice of discipleship. I am confident that what Ken is offering here will become a really helpful and much-needed resource for ongoing reflection and practice for individuals, churches and pioneers.'
Lynn Green, General Secretary of Baptists Together (The Baptist Union of Great Britain)

'*Vital Signs* is an inspiring, thoughtful and refreshingly accessible invitation to whole-life discipleship. I particularly appreciate its breadth – everything from Personal Prayer to Annual Reviews is covered here – and the chapter on 'Times of transition' is simply excellent. I have no doubt that this will become an invaluable resource for individuals and entire communities, helping to create a culture of vibrant Christian transformation.'
Pete Greig, 24-7 Prayer International, and Emmaus Rd Church

'This is such a helpful and timely book for leaders. It offers a holistic and creative approach to integrating discipleship into the whole life of a church in a way that every church leader will find helpful. It brilliantly envisions leaders to see everything in church life as an opportunity for discipleship – even meetings! At a time when church leaders are grappling with how to lead through times of change and complexity in a new cultural moment, this book offers practical and easily implementable ways to do this and to bring clarity and cohesion to church life.'

Rich Johnson, National Leader of New Wine and vicar of All Saints, Worcester

'It's been my privilege to experience Ken's ministry and leadership first hand, both in his church and with other church leaders. And, indeed my own extended family in the city have experienced his pastoral care and support at times of crisis. I've consistently found him to be a thoughtful and strategic leader. This book is packed full of wisdom from decades of church ministry. Ken's heart to equip God's people for works of service jump off each page. I warmly commend this book to you.'

Dr Krish Kandiah OBE, Director Sanctuary Foundation

'*Vital Signs* is indeed a vital handbook for anyone in church leadership of any kind. Whether you lead a small group, a worship team or are seeking to lead and teach in a church setting, this book will be both a blessing and inspiration. Full of practical ideas and prayer prompts, Ken has written a book which helpfully brings together the relationship between whole-life discipleship and the gathered-church community. I highly recommend it.'

Cathy Madavan, author, speaker, and a leaders at Fishponds Baptist Church, Bristol

* * *

About the author

Ken Benjamin is Director of Church Relationships at LICC, UK. Formerly President of Baptists Together (the Baptist Union of Great Britain), and with over 20 years' experience as a senior church minister, he has become a leading voice in the whole-life discipleship movement with a reputation as both a trusted leader and an engaging speaker.

VITAL SIGNS

20 ways to put whole-life discipleship at the heart of your church

Ken Benjamin

INTER-VARSITY PRESS
SPCK Group, Studio 101, The Record Hall, 16–16A Baldwin's Gardens, London
EC1N 7RJ, England
Email: ivp@ivpbooks.com
Website: www.ivpbooks.com

© Ken Benjamin, 2024

Ken Benjamin has asserted his right under the Copyright, Designs and Patents Act
1988 to be identified as Author of this work.

All rights reserved. No part of this publication may be reproduced, stored in a
retrieval system, or transmitted, in any form or by any means, electronic, mechanical,
photocopying, recording or otherwise, without the prior permission of the publisher
or the Copyright Licensing Agency.

Scripture quotations are taken from The Holy Bible, New International Version
(Anglicized edition). Copyright © 1979, 1984, 2011 by Biblica. Used by permission
of Hodder & Stoughton Ltd, an Hachette UK company. All rights reserved. 'NIV' is a
registered trademark of Biblica. UK trademark number 1448790.

First published 2024

British Library Cataloguing-in-Publication Data
A catalogue record for this book is available from the British Library.

ISBN: 978–1–78974–498–9
eBook ISBN: 978–1–78974–499–6

Set in Minion Pro 11/14 pt
Typeset in Great Britain by Fakenham Prepress Solutions, Fakenham, Norfolk
Printed and bound in Great Britain by Clays Ltd, Elcograf S.p.A.

Produced on paper from sustainable sources.

*Inter-Varsity Press publishes Christian books that are true to the Bible and that
communicate the gospel, develop discipleship and strengthen the church for its mission
in the world.*

*IVP originated within the Inter-Varsity Fellowship, now the Universities and Colleges
Christian Fellowship, a student movement connecting Christian Unions in universities
and colleges throughout Great Britain, and a member movement of the International
Fellowship of Evangelical Students. Website: www.uccf.org.uk. That historic association
is maintained, and all senior IVP staff and committee members subscribe to the UCCF
Basis of Faith.*

Contents

Contents

Section 4
WHEN WE RESPOND

Acknowledgements

I much prefer team sports to individual ones. Whether it's tennis doubles or the Ryder Cup, there's something about working together that's more compelling than going it alone. I'm so thankful that producing *Vital Signs* has been a team game from start to finish – a game of multiple teams, in fact.

First, there's my brilliant colleagues on the LICC team, including all our staff and Church Team Associates who have patiently read, reviewed and helped make improvements to this book. Their questions and suggestions have brought greater clarity throughout.

The team at IVP have brought fresh eyes, perceptive edits and much-appreciated encouragements. *Vital Signs* has required a new methodology from both of us, because it isn't a stand-alone text; it's a key element alongside the assessment tool, next steps videos and other insight articles (licc.org.uk/vitalsigns). I'm grateful they've supported this multi-faceted approach.

The biggest team contribution has come from church leaders just like you. The ideas and insights we've distilled into these twenty vital signs come from the thousands of churches and church leaders we've connected with at LICC. We hear new whole-life discipleship stories and insights every time we visit a church or spend time with church leaders. We're also especially thankful for those churches, friends and supporters of LICC whose financial support has made *Vital Signs* possible.

On a personal note, special mention goes to Chichester Baptist Church – the church I had the privilege of serving as minister for almost twenty-five years. They understood and supported my own efforts to lead a whole-life disciplemaking church all that time. My story is inseparable from their story.

Acknowledgements

Finally, I want to dedicate this book to the team that is my family: Zoe, James, Alex, Gabby and Sue. I love being a team with you all. Seeing you work out whole-life discipleship in your own everyday contexts is the greatest of privileges.

Introduction

Why whole-life disciplemaking is vital

Thank you for buying this book. Now let me sell it to you.

Why? Because it will require much more of you than the purchase price. It asks you to consider nothing less than everything in the life of the local church. Whatever your level of leadership, if you take its lessons to heart there will be work to do. But there will also be so much to gain.

Throughout the book, the 'everything' of church life is broken down into twenty different vital signs. In medicine, a vital sign is a clinical measurement that indicates the state of a patient's essential bodily functions. In other words, it's a reliable marker of health – a simple but essential check that points to a wider picture of wellness or illness. If your vital signs look good, the chances are your body is functioning as it should. If, however, they look bad, it is likely you will need treatment or even a lifestyle change. In the same way, the purpose of this book, and the wider suite of resources it sits alongside, is to help you read your church's vital signs so you can accurately assess its health and discern the potential treatment it may need.

This book is for anyone with a leadership role in their church. This very definitely includes any pastoral staff, but it's also for voluntary leaders, worship leaders, small-group leaders and so on. If you have any leadership responsibility in your church and you're going to commit to considering these twenty vital signs of church life, you need to know up front that the commitment is worth it. So, let's put it this way: these are the vital signs of a church that is growing whole-life disciples of Jesus Christ, and this task is essential.

It's not about just running services, operating community initiatives, playing music, hosting groups or making meals, as wonderful as all those things are. It's not about just 'doing church', in fact; it's about equipping and inspiring people to join in God's mission in every single part of their lives *outside* the building. This book is specifically about establishing a church culture that nurtures disciples who are learning from and living for Jesus in everything they do – Monday to Saturday, as well as Sunday; at work, at home and at play, as well as at church – engaging in God's mission when they're scattered, as well as when they're gathered.

Here are three reasons why this is truly vital, any one of which might be particularly critical for you and your church at this time.

1 *Growing whole-life disciples is missionally vital.* Right now, there are some great stories of church growth in the UK for which we can thank God. But overall, the UK church is ageing and declining, and we simply can't be OK with that. Former Executive Director of the London Institute for Contemporary Christianity (LICC) Mark Greene wrote in his foundational essay, *Imagine How We Can Reach the UK*: 'The UK will never be reached until we create open, authentic, learning and praying communities focused on making whole-life disciples, who take the opportunities to show and share the gospel wherever they relate to people in their daily lives.'[1]

   In other words, if God's people are only equipped to join in his mission through church-run activities, an awful lot of their lives is lying fallow. There is a desperate need to prioritise helping Christians understand and embrace the call to join in his redemptive work through their every task, conversation and relationship.

2 *A fuller understanding of discipleship is vital.* Many UK churches experiencing growth approach LICC for help when it comes to nurturing disciples. They tell us people are finding their way into church and faith in Jesus, but it's a struggle to help them grow beyond that point. They have questions

about how to help Christians in their daily lives as followers of Jesus. This is what being a disciple should be all about, but so often we, as the UK church, have narrowed the meaning of discipleship. Sometimes we've used the word to refer to a specific, boxed-off discipleship course, or to implement certain spiritual disciplines, or we've unintentionally implied that it's a 'next level' stage for super-keen Christians.

In Jesus' day, a disciple was first and foremost an apprentice, a learner, someone trying to follow the way of their rabbi in all of life. So the concept of 'whole-life discipleship' used in this book is not a new invention; it's an attempt to recapture the truth of what discipleship always meant. When people take that vision to heart, it transforms everything.

3 *Discipleship is a vital and often missing element for the emerging generations in our churches.* The message of whole-life discipleship is vital for all people, but LICC's research conversations with millennials and Gen Z have revealed their particular yearning for a holistic understanding of the gospel. These are the generations leaving the church at the fastest rate. We so often find they're not running away because they don't believe. Instead, they're drifting away because they don't see the relevance of faith to their everyday lives. They are looking for an integrated way of life that empowers them to be consistent in values and action in every area of life – and therefore to be authentic. That is precisely the kind of life Jesus lived and wants for us all, and precisely what we mean by whole-life discipleship.

Once we're convinced that whole-life discipleship is vital and we begin to emphasise it in our churches, the implications for church life ripple out to pretty much everything we do, with implications too for every kind of leader. The desire to make whole-life disciples affects the whole life of the church and the whole life of the church leader. In essence, building a whole-life disciplemaking church means looking at every aspect of our communal life and our role as leaders and asking the challenging question: 'Are we making disciples here?' If we're not (or at least not as effectively as we could do), the next step is to ask what changes we could make to change the answer to a firmer 'yes'.

That, in a nutshell, is what this book and its accompanying *Vital Signs Assessment Tool* (see page 11 for more on this) will help you do. As you read the chapters, you'll discover insights to help you move from good intentions to best practice and ensure the gathered life of your church equips your people for all of life, every day of the week. As a whole, this project draws on LICC's work with thousands of churches over more than forty years, and my own experience leading a local church for twenty-five years and as a former president of the Baptist Union of Great Britain. The wisdom distilled here comes from listening to what's genuinely helped the thousands of church leaders we've connected with during that time. John Stott, who founded LICC in 1982, said that 'every true disciple is a listener' and challenged us all to engage in 'triple listening' – paying attention simultaneously to God's word, the world around us and one another, combining the insights derived from all three.[2] The advice given for each vital sign therefore comes from our best efforts at triple listening, and the stories shared are real examples of what this actually looks like (with some name and place changes).

From all that listening, one key finding has shaped this book more than any other. Church leaders tell us time and again that simply having good intentions is not enough. When we add 'making whole-life disciples' to our already-full to-do list, it may feature for a while, but it will never become a long-term emphasis in our churches. Or worse, we may drift into feeling as though we've 'done' whole-life discipleship because we ran a single series or event on it several years ago. Instead, for whole-life disciplemaking to survive in our churches, it must be more than just another good idea that slips away from our priorities. It must be embedded rather than added; built in rather than bolted on.

For tired, overworked church leaders (you may identify with that description), this is good news. Know now that this book's message is emphatically *not* that we all need to do lots of new things. Instead, it's that we need to continue doing some of the things we already do in new and refreshing ways, with a discipleship edge to them. We've found that when this approach is followed, the effect is life-changing and lasting – not only for congregations and church leaders, but for the individuals, organisations and communities we seek to serve beyond the gathered church.

What we have offered here, therefore, is intended as a helpful checklist rather than a burdensome to-do list. The aim is not to make you feel guilty about areas where you need to see change, but to highlight straightforward ways to make gains in the season ahead. You don't have to be thriving in all twenty areas to make good progress. Every small gain found in any of these chapters towards the vital goal of whole-life disciplemaking is worth celebrating.

At the same time, don't be fooled by the simplicity of the tried-and-tested changes described in each chapter. Whole-life discipleship can be simple to understand but challenging to implement. Without careful attention to detail and a nuanced approach, too many Christians in UK churches can still totally miss what it is to be a whole-life disciple, and our churches can totally miss the opportunities to equip them for it.

I also recognise that embarking on a project to embed a new central value in your church culture can be a daunting prospect. As we've worked on whole-life disciplemaking with church leaders across the UK, two concerns have come up regularly. It's worth mentioning these now, in case either applies to you.

First, some church leaders worry that if they emphasise the importance of life beyond the gathered church, their people will volunteer for and attend church activities less often. At a time when it's increasingly hard to recruit the needed volunteers for important church roles, they naturally question whether focusing on mission that happens outside the church programme is timely or wise. But in truth, what we're advocating here is an emphasis on scattered ministry *alongside*, not instead of, gathered ministry. While sometimes we do need to ask the important questions ('Are we spending too much time together in church at the expense of time with others? Is our programme too full?'), experience shows that concerns about the impact of a whole-life disciplemaking culture on attendance and volunteering are often misplaced. In my own church, and in the churches I've visited for LICC, I've genuinely found people often become more motivated to attend and serve in a church that values everything they do and prioritises equipping them for the whole of their lives.

Second, some church leaders worry that the emphasis whole-life discipleship places on the practical outworking of our faith might leave less room for theological reflection. But as you read each chapter of this book, you'll see this fear is unwarranted. Just as the gathered and scattered aspects of church life complement one another, so too do the practical and theological aspects of our discipleship.

Finally, a note on the structure of the chapters in this book. Each chapter addresses a particular vital sign – an area of church life that indicates how we're doing with disciplemaking. These are grouped into four sections. 'When it's just us' looks at the elements of church leadership that happen when we're on our own, or at least when most people in our church won't be together observing what we're doing. This includes aspects from personal prayer to one-on-one pastoral work. 'When we gather' deals with the main group activities of the church, from services to small groups and beyond. 'When we plan' explores the crucial role of team meetings in the culture of the church. Finally, 'When we respond' looks at the occasional but significant moments that crop up in the life of every church, including times of transition, crisis and accidental encounters. You can read each chapter in order from start to finish or jump back and forth to chapters of particular interest. Every chapter starts with a simple 'in a nutshell' summary to help you quickly get to the heart of the matter and closes with a simple prayer, because nothing good happens in our churches and in our disciplemaking endeavours if prayer isn't fuelling it.

As you embark on your journey, may our Lord work through this book to speak directly to you. May he help you to discern key lessons and next steps for you and your church. And in our churches, neighbourhoods, workplaces, leisure places and beyond, may he bring about nothing less than transformation – through the impact of faithful whole-life disciples of Jesus.

Key terms in this book

Over the years, LICC has coined some helpful phrases to communicate some vital truths. Here's a handy guide to some important words and phrases you'll come across in this book.

Whole-life discipleship

A whole-life disciple is someone learning to follow the way of Jesus in their place at this time. Of course, there's no such thing as part-time discipleship, but the inclusion of the term 'whole-life' emphasises that following Jesus includes absolutely every aspect of a Christian's life. It all matters to God – our work, our relationships, our hobbies, our leisure, our expenditure, our conversations. He invites us to join in his redemptive purposes in all of it. Any implication that our mission as Christians is primarily carried out through church-run activities is a diminishing of this essential truth.

The sacred–secular divide

The sacred–secular divide is the all-too-common belief that some parts of our life are 'sacred' or 'spiritual' and therefore really important to God (prayer, Sunday services, church-based activities), while others are 'secular' and therefore irrelevant to God (work, school, university, sport, the arts, music, rest, sleep, hobbies and so on). Though it often springs from well-meaning teaching, it's a lie that distorts God's character and severely limits our everyday enjoyment of him. Tragically, it also severely limits our understanding of our everyday role in God's purposes. Because of this sacred–secular divide, far too many Christians don't feel equipped for mission in their daily context, or helped to know Christ's presence with them in a way that means they represent him well, wherever they spend most of their time.

The gathered and scattered church

We are the church when we gather together on Sunday mornings or weekday evenings. And we are equally the church when we are scattered in our everyday places, Monday to Saturday. The one setting informs the other: what happens in services and midweek groups equips and sustains us for the opportunities and challenges we meet in the places we find ourselves in each day.

Your frontline

Every Christian has a 'frontline': a place or activity where regular time is spent with people who don't follow Jesus. They're places God has called us to – places of possibility and potential, where he works through us to make himself known to others and to bless them (see the 6Ms of fruitfulness below for more on how this looks). It could be a job, a gym, a pub, a sports team, a home, a cycling group, the corner shop, an amateur dramatic society; it could be our family – the list goes on. Whether we're old or young, healthy or infirm, employed or not, we all have a frontline.

The 6Ms of fruitfulness

One of the great joys of being a Christian is realising that God chooses to work in and through us, wherever we are. One of the harder things, though, is being able to spot how and where this happens. Many of us just don't have the eyes to see how we're already being fruitful with Jesus in our daily lives. The 6Ms of fruitfulness are a framework to help us see how God is already working through us, and to inspire our imagination for how he could in future. Each of us has the opportunity to:

- *Model godly character*: the fruit of the Spirit (Galatians 5:22–23) at work in our actions, words and thoughts;
- *Make good work*: doing everything to and for the glory of God;
- *Minister grace and love*: going the extra mile for others;
- *Mould culture*: finding ways to make changes for the better;

- *be a Mouthpiece for truth and justice*: combatting lies, snuffing out gossip and working for justice;
- *be a Messenger of the gospel*: sharing the hope we have in Jesus and the difference he makes in our lives.

Making the most of *Vital Signs*

Vital Signs is more than just this book!

It also includes a free online assessment tool, next steps videos, and insight articles that'll help you identify what your church is doing well, where you need to improve, and the practical things you can do to embed whole-life discipleship more deeply in your church.

If you've not taken the assessment yet, this is a great time to do it. It's a quick process – no more than 15 minutes – but it'll give you detailed insights on how you're getting on with each of the vital signs covered in this book. Simply answer 20 multiple-choice questions and you'll receive a tailored report giving you a score in each of the four sections ('When it's just us', 'When we gather', 'When we plan' and 'When we respond) as well as for each vital sign, and written analysis of what your scores mean. Then you can dive into the particular chapters of this book that are highlighted as key areas for you to make progress in – or just read the whole thing cover to cover.

Alongside the book and the assessment tool, you can explore implications and actions for your church by watching the short next steps videos and reading helpful articles that unpack how different areas of your church life can equip people for ministry in daily life.

Finally, you'll get the most value from *Vital Signs* if you take the assessment with your whole leadership team, receiving a group score and analysis that you can discuss and plan from. You could make it an annual routine, benchmarking against your previous scores and tracking your progress.

Find it all at **licc.org.uk/vitalsigns** or scan the QR code.

Section 1

WHEN IT'S JUST US

Vital sign 1
Daily prayers

In a nutshell

In our 'just me and God' moments, it's good for our prayers to touch on the details of people's ordinary lives. Over time, we may have developed – or fallen into – a formula for our private prayers. Consider where that formula includes space to focus on the way discipleship plays out in normal life, as well as big life events and church-based activities.

As church leaders, no one in our church family ever contacts us to let us know they're having an average day, do they?

Admittedly, we don't want everyone in our church to contact us every single day with the news that nothing newsworthy is happening. But the reality is that our people tend to call us about the extraordinary rather than the ordinary. We'll get a call or message when something is going extremely well or, perhaps more frequently, when it's going extremely badly. Of course we want to hear the big stuff, even if it's difficult. Whether it's good, bad or uncertain news, it's a privilege to be there for our people at these times. Having insight into some of the most significant moments of someone's life and praying for them at these pivotal times is precious.

But at the same time, if we only hear about these extreme times, there's a danger that we can end up with a skewed view of life. If our phone calls and inboxes are filled with these major news items, we can end up disproportionately leading, preaching about and equipping our people for the extremes of life. But most days, most of our people aren't experiencing those extremes. As leaders, the largest part of our disciplemaking challenge is how we equip people who are not critically ill today, who are not facing redundancy, who have not just got engaged, who are not planning a baptism ... but instead are having an average day in their everyday place. In those regular days, their challenge is to imagine what Jesus would do if he was living their life; to ask, 'What does it look like to be a faithful follower of Jesus where I find myself today?'

It's easy to think that crises are the key times for spiritual growth. There's no doubt they offer discipleship learning opportunities. But we can so easily underestimate the spiritual lessons that come from our everyday lives. The days that would never make it into a biography, that wouldn't even make it into a social media post, still contain opportunities and challenges to grow as a disciple. As Edwin and Lillian Harvey write in their book *The Christian's Daily Challenge*:

> We think that conspicuous events, striking experiences, exalted moments have most to do with our character and capacity. We are wrong. Common days, monotonous hours, wearisome paths, plain old tools, and everyday clothes tell the real story. Good habits are not made on birthdays, nor Christian character at the new year. The workshop of character is everyday life.[1]

So, what does all this mean for our daily prayers? In essence, it's easy to fill our prayers with the things that fill our phone screens, newsfeeds and inboxes, with no thought for the things that don't scream for our attention. If we only hear of extreme life headlines, we're less likely to pray for everyday frontlines – the ordinary places where people spend time with those who don't follow Jesus. And if no one calls us to say they're having an average day, there's a real danger that we never pray for those average days that make up the vast majority of our people's lives.

I know this all too well from experience. When I pray, I usually try to start by giving God thanks and praise. Then I'll typically pray for major national and global issues, the overseas missionaries our church supports, upcoming events in church, and people in my church who are experiencing a crisis. There's nothing in this list I would want to drop. It's right to pray for all these things. But how often do I pray for most of my congregation in how they spend most of their time – working, doing the housework, ferrying kids about, meeting friends for a run, playing music, spending time with their spouses and so on? That question is a constant challenge to me, but I'm excited to imagine the impact if more of our prayers included this everyday element more often.

If we're going to start regularly including this everyday element in our prayers, good intentions aren't enough on their own. I've certainly found that I'm not always good at this, so if that applies to you too, you're not alone. I need regular prompts to change my established prayer patterns. In my own prayer life as a church leader, two simple practices helped:

Real-world reminders

As a minister in the same church for more than twenty years, I had a ten-minute walk from my house to work. On the walk, I passed the houses of some of the people in my church, and I tried to use those particular houses as a prompt to pray for all the people in my church, wherever they were going to be that day. For me, visual clues as simple as walking past someone's house helped change my prayer habit.

If I had that same walk today, I would take those visual reminders a step further. The people in the houses I'd pass are all at different ages and stages: a retired couple, a single person working in a challenging NHS job and a family with university-aged children. So the walk could act as a reminder to pray about a whole range of different circumstances as I pass each house.

Digital reminders

During my years in church leadership, I would often change the desktop image on my computer to keep it fresh and remind me to pray for the everyday discipleship of those in my church. An aerial picture of the area, for example, or a local landmark where lots of people had their frontlines – a business park, a shopping centre or the local university. It's a simple thing, but it helped me keep those everyday places at the front of my mind.

What would it look like for you to include simple prompts like these in your daily pattern to help you incorporate people's ordinary lives in your prayers? Perhaps you could go to the list of people in your church, pick one or two people and ask God to prompt you to pray for the opportunities and challenges they encounter on their frontlines today, believing that your prayers make a difference. Or you could drop them a text or an email simply saying, 'I'm praying for you today. How can I pray?'

Sometimes people will be able to answer that question easily. At other times, a more detailed prompt will help, like asking about the 'presence', 'pressure' and 'purpose' in their day. These three topics can easily prompt us to know how to pray.

- *Presence* – how do you see God working on your frontline? How do you see his presence in the ordinary places you go?
- *Pressure* – are there any challenging situations on your frontline at the moment?
- *Purpose* – what opportunities do you have to join in with God's purposes on your frontline, in the things you do, the words you say and the way you act?

Of course, we should ask these questions in a way that doesn't add guilt to anyone who doesn't have a clear answer. Even when they don't have answers, asking the questions can encourage them to think about what it means to be a disciple on their frontline. In many ways, not having an answer, particularly to the 'presence' and 'purpose' questions, is also a prompt for our prayers. And equally, sometimes the answers to these questions will fuel our prayers with reasons for joyful thanksgiving.

Once we've started to embed these 'everyday' topics in our prayer life, there's also a teaching opportunity in explaining it to others. Jesus modelled this when he prayed for the raising of Lazarus (admittedly a far from average day!). It seems as though he prayed out loud so that others would gain from eavesdropping: *'Father, I thank you that you have heard me. I knew that you always hear me, but I said this for the benefit of the people standing here, that they may believe that you sent me'* (John 11:41–42).

In a similar way, when we admit that we need visual prompts to remind us to pray for everyday issues, this helps others to consider doing the same. When we explain that as a small-group leader, youth leader or church leader we love to pray for our people's ordinary days as well as their extraordinary days, it's much more likely others will do the same, for themselves and their friends too.

It's no accident that our first vital sign is about personal daily prayers, and the next is about personal Bible reading. All the other signs will be more public, more noticeable. But none of the others will be truly effective if our personal prayer and Bible reading is out of step. A hunger for prayer has been a hallmark preceding every great move of God, so in this case our persistent prayers should be for the impact our people can have in their ordinary places and through their daily tasks. Those kinds of prayers are the foundation for truly equipping our people to live out their faith in all the details of daily life. When we regularly bring those details to the Lord, it shapes our thinking – and the results of our prayers can be so much more wonderful than we realise. As John Wesley is frequently quoted as saying, 'Prayer is where the action is.'[2]

Pray about it

Lord of all things, as I pray today I'm picturing the faces of my church family and their everyday places. I lift up to you the places where they'll be – schools, hospitals, factories, offices, farms, shops, universities, care homes, warehouses, building sites, leisure places, homes and beyond.

Some are busy and some are bored, some are blessed and some are burdened. Please encourage them and work through them all today. In their everyday opportunities and challenges, guide and strengthen them.

Is there anyone I should particularly pray for or send a message to? Please guide my thoughts to them now. Amen.

Vital sign 2
Daily Bible reading

In a nutshell

We can read the Bible for many reasons, but primarily we read it as followers of Jesus seeking to become more mature disciples. As church leaders, it's vital to seek out biblical insights, stories, implications and applications that will help us to both live more like Jesus in our own daily lives and equip others to do the same.

If you like, we can arm-wrestle over the order of these first two chapters. I'm not making the case that daily prayer is more vital than daily Bible reading or vice versa. But I am strongly suggesting that both should come before all the other vital signs of a frontline-friendly church. These two daily practices provide the vital building blocks for everything else. Quite simply, if we pray more often for people's daily lives, and if we also regularly read the Bible with our eyes open to its implications for every part of life, all the other vital signs in this book should follow. Equally, if either of these two vital signs is missing, all the other habits and actions this book describes will run out of energy, and we might not even notice when they're lacking.

We don't just read the Bible because it's the right thing to do. We should read with a hunger to genuinely encounter the living God and his teaching. Yet for most of us, daily Bible reading isn't easy. If you're one of the exceptions – someone who finds daily Bible reading easy, genuinely keeps on track with reading the Bible and applying the lessons to your day, and breezily discovers one flowing application and blessing after another – then please bear with the rest of us. There should still be something in this chapter for you, but it's written especially for those who struggle, because many of us find daily Bible reading to be a complex mix of competing thoughts. Rather than settling, our minds fill with almost any thought except the text in front of us. We think up issues, interruptions, problems and distractions. We mentally wander off.

And yet we also believe that persevering with daily Bible reading is worth it – and more than worth it; vital, you might say. We need good habits when it comes to personal Bible reading, because a whole-life approach to discipleship should affect *our* whole lives as well as the whole lives of the churches we lead. In other words, we need to be seeking biblical wisdom for the tasks, places and relationships that make up our own and our people's ordinary schedules.

While this book is for all kinds of church leader, from senior ministers to small-group leaders, there's an extra factor to navigate here for those of us who preach or teach from the Bible. As a preacher myself, one danger I find with personal daily Bible reading is that as soon as I've got an insight, my mind is trying to work it into a sermon. The sermon might well be the right place to share that fresh thought or insight, but sometimes God wants to use it to speak to me personally. In fact, when it comes to Bible reading, we will usually need to take it personally before we take it to anyone else. Some days, taking it personally for our own whole-life discipleship journey is all that's required. Of course, the more we develop this helpful habit of finding personal whole-life connections, the more likely we'll be able to see connections for others in our preaching. In that sense the two can go together. Bible reading helps us all recalibrate back to our Maker's settings for the day ahead. In a world of competing stories, the Bible reminds us of the way things really are and should be, so we can find our role in God's world.

LICC's research shows that churches that have managed to embed whole-life disciplemaking in their culture over several years consistently keep the Bible central and connect it to everyday life. This is seen and noticed publicly in preaching and teaching, but it must also flow out of the leaders' private Bible reading. As one church leader in the research describes it:

Scripture is the starting point for all aspects of discipleship. The whole way I read Scripture is through this whole-life discipleship lens. Jesus came to make disciples, and he sent us out to make disciples, and we have God's word to help us be disciples and to make disciples. I guess all my reading of Scripture is through that lens.[1]

Some people suspect that if our churches focus more on the lives people live during the week, it will somehow detract from the centrality of the Bible. But in fact the opposite is true. LICC's research shows that the more churches focus on equipping people to live out their faith on their daily frontlines, the more they recognise how essential the Bible is in helping Christians be more Christ-like. And that, in turn, leads to a deeper love for the Bible.

So, what exactly does reading the Bible with a whole-life perspective look like? In essence, it means learning to recognise the implications of Scripture for our place in God's world, wherever we find ourselves Monday to Saturday, as well as Sunday. Looking for this 'whole-life' edge is vital. Of course we should acknowledge that it's not always easy, but there are steps we can all take to discover it. The Bible is full of frontline implications, and we can get to them in any given passage by asking three simple questions:

- What did it mean then?
- What does it mean now?
- So what?

The first two of these questions may feel like more familiar territory than the last. We may be used to unpacking the meaning of a passage for its original readers and for us today. In some passages this process is more straightforward than in others, of course. In Old Testament passages, the 'What does it mean now?' step should include what we now know and have been shown in the light of Jesus. Commentaries and devotional guides often help us with these first two steps. We are often less used to joining the dots to the 'So what?' for our circumstances today and tomorrow. Conversely, there's a danger that we jump straight to a presumed 'So what?', particularly with very well-known passages, without taking the time to check it against the meaning of the text. And, of course, in case this seems like a simple functional tick-list, over and above these three steps we are depending on the living God guiding and speaking to us through his Spirit.

Let's consider Nehemiah 8 as a worked example. The chapter describes God's word being read to 'the assembly' – the people of Israel. Although this is a public reading of just the first five books of the Old Testament, the whole-life lessons we can draw out also apply to personal reading of the whole Bible, particularly the expectation that God will speak through his word. In the passage, both the people and the teachers of the law know these words are useful to their lives. The teachers are prepared to do the work needed to spell out their contemporary relevance (What did it mean then? and What does it mean now?), and the people are then willing to do something about it (So what?).

If we include another simple framework, we can also see a 'head, heart and hands' approach to reading Scripture in Nehemiah 8.

Head

While they are reading, Ezra and the teachers of the law work to make sure there is understanding: *'They read from the Book of the Law of God, making it clear and giving the meaning so that the people understood what was being read'* (Nehemiah 8:8).

The texts being read were in Hebrew, but by this time a good number of the audience were likely to be more familiar with Aramaic. Just as we have translations into English, work was required to translate from Hebrew to Aramaic, and then from the Aramaic to a deeper understanding of both the meaning and the 'So what?' for their lives. That deeper understanding is just as crucial for us in our private Bible reading. Commentaries, study notes and apps can all help with this.

Heart

Hearing the word being read is clearly an emotional experience. In verse 9, we read that *'all the people had been weeping as they listened to the words of the Law'*. This is partly because the reading reminds them that they have failed to live up to the standards required. Yet later, in verse 12, there is *'great joy, because they now understood the words that had been made known to them'*.

What is clear is that reading Scripture can and should be an emotionally moving experience and helps develop a healthy character, more tuned in to the will of God. Our emotions often drive our actions: if we allow ourselves to feel deeply the meaning of a passage, we're much more likely to put the 'So what?' into practice. We can sometimes be a bit suspicious of emotions when it comes to understanding the Bible, but the truth is that our emotions often drive our actions. So when we allow ourselves to be moved deeply by God and his word, we are often much more likely to put the 'So what?' into practice.

Hands

Indeed, it would be a great shame if all we gained from reading the Bible was head knowledge and a heart response. But more than that happens in this passage. The chapter goes on to say that the following day, the people discovered they were supposed to be celebrating a particular festival they had neglected (Nehemiah 8:13–14). A key part of this *'festival of the seventh month'* was the inclusion of *'those who have nothing prepared'*, which almost certainly means those who had nothing. Reading Scripture recalibrated the people towards the way they should be living, including remembering that God was concerned for the poor, the widowed, the fatherless, the orphaned and those among them from elsewhere – strangers and outsiders.

Together, the two frameworks we've just explored provide a really helpful foundation for noticing and internalising the

Bible's whole-life implications, but there are other helpful points to consider as we go. First, we should be aware of the style or genre we are reading. Famously, 2 Timothy 3:16–17 says: *'All Scripture is God-breathed and is useful for teaching, rebuking, correcting and training in righteousness, so that the servant of God may be thoroughly equipped for every good work.'* But that doesn't mean all Scripture is equally easy to interpret or should be interpreted in the same way. We need to take a little time to consider how the genre we're reading affects its meaning – if it's Daniel or Revelation, for example, we'll need to approach it differently from a letter like Romans or Hebrews.

Second, I'm always keen to find a takeaway thought for the day, but that kind of thought is spelled out more clearly in some passages than in others. Sometimes there won't be a neatly packaged buzz phrase. Sometimes we'll pick up the passage's place in the bigger biblical story, and that's enough. When looking for a takeaway, we should also be aware of when we're zooming in to detail and when we're zooming out. It's good to notice and be blessed by a tiny detail that we've not noticed before, but we shouldn't do this at the expense of noticing the big thing going on in the passage and its part in the bigger story of the Bible. Put another way, we should always be wary of making a lot of a little. Keeping an eye to the big thing going on helps us keep specific verses in perspective. So, for example, if I'm reading Jesus and Peter's exchange in Matthew 14:30–32, I might come away with the takeaway phrase 'Why did you doubt?', but I shouldn't forget that while Jesus asks this, he's walking on water – and so, for that matter, is Peter.

For some of us, asking useful questions of ourselves might help clarify things. For example:

- What's going on in my day today?
- Is there one thing on my mind that this passage might help me address?
- Is there a specific thing I can do based on my reading today – an attitude to lean in to, an action to take?
- How will I take this passage and apply it to myself today?

When we ask these questions, we should be careful not to be too formulaic. Not every day's Bible reading need necessarily lead to an everyday application. We may not see the return today, but there is an accumulation over time as we are saturated by God's word and learn to listen out for his voice.

Above all, when we read the Bible we should be looking for the 'So what?' What are the implications and applications of the day's reading? Those 'So whats?' will illuminate our path as whole-life disciples for the day ahead. When we 'bring out the book', as Nehemiah puts it, let's take it personally, for all aspects of our lives.

Pray about it

Lord, when I read the Bible, please help me to join up the dots. Help me to learn what the passage meant then, what it means now and how the 'So what?' should be applied by your disciples today, starting with me.

Help me to find the connections between your word and your world today. Amen.

Vital sign 3
Leading by example

In a nutshell

While every chapter in this book considers different vital signs of healthy whole-life discipleship in the church, we as leaders are supposed to be a living vital sign for others. To help others see their lives through a whole-life lens, we need to show that we clearly believe in whole-life discipleship ourselves, seeking to live in a way that practises what we preach.

Every church seeking to embed whole-life disciplemaking in its culture goes through the same five-step journey. It looks like this:

1 *Convince*: we start by becoming convinced that whole-life discipleship is vital for every Christian and that it is often missing in UK churches. (If you're not convinced yet, look back to page 2–3 for three reasons why you should be!)
2 *Commence*: we then make a start on some of the vital signs discussed in this book.
3 *Commit*: once we've made a start, the next stage is to prioritise whole-life disciplemaking. It must become one of the key values in the life of the church, or else the moves we make towards it will be no more than token gestures rather than a genuine change of posture.
4 *Re-commit*: even with that resolve, whole-life disciplemaking can so easily slip away from our priorities. Every church will go through stages when it needs reminders and seasons of recommitting.
5 *Commend*: whole-life discipleship isn't a niche pursuit for

just a few churches. It's for our whole village, town or city, for the other churches in our denomination or stream, for all Christians. Once we have embedded a whole-life disciplemaking culture and seen the fruit of it, we will want to commend it to others.

These five steps apply just as much to us as individual church leaders as they do to whole churches. In fact, the first four affect our ability as leaders to do the fifth – to commend whole-life discipleship to our people. Let's walk through how each step applies to us in our role as church leaders.

First, if we want to be effective in commending whole-life discipleship to others in our church, we need to ask: have we personally become *convinced* of the need for whole-life discipleship? LICC's research into churches that have maintained a focus on whole-life discipleship for at least five years shows that leaders must be convinced in order for the culture to stick.[1] The helpful term the research report used for this was that the leaders have reached a 'theological point of no return'. They're thoroughly convicted that making whole-life disciples is a biblical and missional imperative – not just a nice-to-have or termly theme. The principles of whole-life discipleship are biblical principles. Sometimes, leaders who have become convinced through hearing an LICC speaker or using one of our resources have told us that it's now 'difficult to think of discipleship in any other way'. Or, as another leader put it when asked why they had a whole-life take on discipleship: 'My question would be, what's the alternative? Part-time discipleship?'

Second, have we *commenced* the journey of whole-life discipleship for ourselves? Do we know where our own frontlines are – the ordinary places where we regularly spend time among those who don't follow Jesus, including outside of our church programme? And do we prayerfully view our discipleship as including every aspect of our lives, rather than just the 'holy' or church-based parts? There's a particular danger that those of us in church leadership may compartmentalise our faith in our minds, unconsciously limiting our view of mission to the things we do in that leadership role. We need to acknowledge God's intense interest in our free time, our work and our relationships beyond church – all of these are opportunities to join his work in the world.

Third, have we *committed* to and prioritised our own whole-life discipleship? If so, it will be reflected in the way we personally read the Bible and pray, as we saw in the first two chapters, and it will spill out into the way we live. The theologian Richard Foster gives a helpful perspective here. Although he's best known for his work on spiritual practices and disciplines, he has also made clear that the prayer and study he advocates sits in the context of our everyday lives and reality:

> Some people who read my books are surprised to learn that I had never been drawn to a monastic life, as important and valuable as that way of life is. For me, the greatest challenge has always been to experience the reality of God in the midst of going to work and raising the kids and cleaning the house and paying the bills.[2]

Fourth, have we *re-committed* to whole-life discipleship when it has dropped off our radar? Even with the best of plans and intentions, whole-life discipleship can imperceptibly slip down the priority list. If we've been through one of those seasons when other things have dominated our waking hours, we need to prayerfully review and ask God to help us reset our perspective. Not that we should feel guilty for not ticking a box marked 'frontline mission' and should now put it back on our to-do list, but we need his help to remember that he's working in all the details of our lives, as well as the big things that shout for our attention.

Finally, when we can answer these first four questions positively, we will be best placed to *commend* whole-life discipleship to the people in our churches whose care is entrusted to us. Before they hear our words about the call to whole-life discipleship, people will look at our lives and notice whether we practise what we preach.

Of course, our need to set an example has been perfectly modelled for all of us by Jesus. Jesus' whole life embodied and demonstrated the truth of his words. Paul clearly adhered to this way of teaching too, and so it remains a pattern for us in turn to emulate.

In Titus 2:7–8, Paul sets out the agenda for Titus to be an example in everything he does: *'In everything set them an example by doing what is good. In your teaching show integrity, seriousness and soundness of speech that cannot be condemned, so that those who oppose you may be ashamed because they have nothing bad to say about us.'* When he mentions the verbal teaching Titus will offer to others, he underlines that his words should be characterised by integrity, without any corruption. Put simply, as leaders our words should be matched by our actions, so that those who might stand against the message of Jesus have *'nothing bad to say about us'.*

It's also notable that the rest of Titus 2 is full of examples and instructions for the whole of life – not just what happens in the gathered church. Clearly, the need for Titus to model the message is more than theory. Paul gives teaching for a range of people and circumstances, and while the individual instructions are for particular groups, we can surely apply them more widely to our own contexts. We read that we are to live in a way that's *'worthy of respect'*, a *'self-controlled'* way that demonstrates we are *'sound in faith'*, as well as *'in love and in endurance'.* We're not to steal anything, and more generally we're to say no to all ungodliness, instead showing we can be *'fully trusted … eager to do what is good'.* In short, we are to *'be reverent'* in the way we live, so that in every way we will make the teaching about God our Saviour attractive. While Paul is giving these instructions to Titus to pass on for his particular context, he is also instructing him to model the kind of life he is promoting. That same lesson applies to all of us as church leaders.

For Ebi, the pastor of a church in north London with a majority African-heritage congregation, embedding whole-life discipleship has meant embracing the fact that he is bi-vocational. Because as well as being a pastor, Ebi is a geography teacher in a large, multicultural secondary school. Before becoming convinced of the whole-life view of discipleship, he viewed this teaching role as just something he had to do to put food on the table and help provide for his family. Now, though, he's increasingly seeing the deep worth of that role and the way it strengthens his pastoral role. He is able to give examples of his own efforts to represent Jesus well at school and speak about how his so-called secular work matters to God. He's no longer praying for the day the church finances will be sufficient for him to drop the school role. Perhaps God is calling him to this workplace for the foreseeable future? Since thinking and praying about whole-life discipleship more carefully, Ebi now has a clearer theology of education and geography, and he wants a similar revelation for those in his church: a keen sense of why their particular work matters to God.

For those in church leadership but not employed by the church (most worship leaders, small-group leaders, those serving on leadership teams and so on), the same lessons Ebi learned can also apply. If our paid employment is our primary frontline, we are well placed to speak from experience. And for those of us in full-time, church-paid roles, the lesson is not to go part time and look for a second job. Instead, it's about finding frontlines outside of the gathered church programme – somewhere we can go regularly and engage with those who don't follow Jesus.

For many of us, this will involve committing to neighbourhood, social or sporting interests away from church. Sometimes that can be very hard to do; life is busy and we'll need to work to preserve these frontlines away from gathered-church contexts. But if we make that effort, it's so good both for our faith and for our mental well-being. Church life can be so all-consumingly busy that we're often tempted to give ourselves an exemption from the general idea of frontline ministry, but others will see whether we are prioritising our own frontlines and whole-life discipleship or not. If we skip these lessons for ourselves, we run the risk of carrying planks in our eyes while pointing out the specks of dust in other people's!

And again, if all that sounds like just another thing to add to your already overflowing to-do list, remember that our frontline stories don't have to be dramatic. Susanna Wesley (mother of Charles and John) wrote this regular prayer, offering all the 'happening of her life to God':

Help me, Lord, to remember that religion is not to be confined to the church, or closet, nor exercised only in prayer and meditation, but that everywhere I am in Your presence. So may my every word and action have a moral content. May all the happenings of my life prove useful and beneficial to me. May all things instruct me and afford me an opportunity of exercising some virtue and daily learning and growing toward Your likeness.[3]

It's also worth remembering that we don't have to pretend to be perfect whole-life disciples or the best in our church on our frontlines, if that were possible. If our words are to have the integrity Paul calls for in Titus 2, we can sometimes encourage others just as much by admitting our mistakes and insecurities as we can by recounting any successes.

Pray about it

Lord, please remind me of my own role as a vital sign of whole-life discipleship for others. May my life increasingly match my words. Please help me to represent you well on my frontlines and to love the people you have placed me alongside there. Amen.

Vital sign 4
Pastoral care

In a nutshell

When we talk of pastoring or pastoral care, my first thought is often about caring for people in their times of difficulty. This is essential, but if it's where our thoughts remain, we risk underplaying the role pastoring can play in all of life's details. Pastoring means being a shepherd for our flock every day, not just on extreme days.

Don't rule yourself out of the lessons in this chapter just because you're not the pastor (or vicar, or minister, or whatever the senior role is called in your church), or you feel your role isn't particularly pastoral. The ministry of pastoring involves a far greater number of people than we might first envisage, and the role of pastor covers more aspects than we often imagine. In this chapter, we'll consider intentional pastoral work, which simply means the times when we set out to do something pastoral. Put simply, if you've deliberately spent time with someone with the intention of encouraging, equipping and supporting them, then this chapter absolutely applies to you. (And in case you're concerned that I've forgotten pastoring isn't all pre-planned, rest assured; we'll consider unplanned 'chance encounters' in the next chapter.)

Most churches have a pastoral expectation placed on them. Some people will assess how 'good' our churches are by how much we care for them in their times of greatest need. Their commitment and service in church, and even whether they move on to a different church, can all depend on their perspective on how pastorally caring we are at those crucial times. As a church leader, it's so easy to fall short of the mark, because people rarely tell us (or know) where or what the mark is until after it's been missed. It could be who visits them, how soon after hearing about the need, how frequently, how caringly, how long for and how much they pray.

Clearly, this is a less-than-healthy approach. Pastoring should be about more than a minimum service level in the times of greatest need. 'Emergency' pastoral care is of course absolutely crucial. But our understanding of pastoring must also include pastoral *equipping* for the places where our people spend the most time. As we saw in the first vital sign, pretty much no one is calling us to ask for that kind of equipping. And that means we need to prayerfully ask ourselves how we can wisely spend more time pastorally equipping them for their everyday lives.

The best way to combat an unhelpful or unbalanced pastoral expectation is with consistent biblical explanation and an alternative demonstration of what is genuinely included in the role of pastor. As church leaders, that means we often need to reframe our own thinking. We frequently see pastors as key carers in the time of greatest need, but we're less likely to see them as principal cheerleaders in the time of greatest opportunity. There's also a danger that we see pastors as primarily concerned with *spiritual* equipping, particularly focused on prayer, Bible reading and church-based service, rather than *whole-life* equipping – helping people put their discipleship into practice day by day.

But in fact, the word 'pastor' comes from the Latin word for shepherd. A pastor is meant to be a shepherd or caretaker of God's flock in all circumstances, not just the extremes. We are given a helpful picture in 1 Peter 5:2–3: *'Be shepherds of God's flock that is under your care, watching over them – not because you must, but because you are willing, as God wants you to be; not pursuing dishonest gain, but eager to serve; not lording it over those entrusted to you, but being examples to the flock.'*

The two phrases *'because you are willing'* and *'eager to serve'* both make clear that the shepherd (pastor) role is driven by a heart that wants the best for others. The phrase *'being examples to the flock'* calls us to model mature discipleship to those we're pastoring, but it also clearly widens the role beyond church activities and times of crisis. It would be absurd to suggest that we should only be an example to people who are sick or jobless, or that the only example we should set is in the way we lead church ministries. This verse points to the whole of our lives. If we're to be examples, it should be for all those entrusted to us, for the whole of their lives – including the way they go about their day-to-day lives, work, relationships, hobbies and beyond.

Church leader, writer and theologian Neil Hudson refers to this as 'moving from a pastoral care contract to a pastoral equipping contract'. Describing his own experience of twenty-five years in church leadership, he says:

> I've had conversations with people that begin with the words, 'It's nothing personal, Neil, but. . .' I always want to stop them and explain that if it's not personal, then I'm probably not the person they should be speaking to. But they seem to want to continue and outline all the issues that they see as problematic in the church and why they are going to leave. And as they draw to the end of their litany of complaint, if they really want to emphasize their unhappiness they will add, 'And above all, you don't care.' And by that point they may be right.

> But in 25 years I've not had someone come and say, 'And above all, you haven't helped me to live well for Christ as a disciple.' It's not that we have always done that particularly well; it's just that it wasn't part of the deal they thought they had signed up for.[1]

Instead, most of the UK church has been built around a deeply held commitment to the pastoral care contract. This is an unspoken and unwritten agreement based on the following simple points:

- It's the task of the leader to be clear about the future vision of the church.

- It's the task of the people to support, invest in and, at least in part, deliver this vision.
- In return, the people will be cared for.

At times, people might test this level of care by absenting themselves from worship, or by not telling anyone that they're ill and then complaining that the minister has not been to visit them. In some cases, the pastoral care contract will be sealed with an unspoken agreement that only a visit from the senior leader is an 'official' church visit. Anyone else does not count. As long as there are vestiges of this pastoral care contract being practised, there will be inherent resistance to the concept of pastoral equipping, of pastoral care that includes (or even focuses on) the frontline ministry of individuals within the church.

In larger churches, it's normal for the task of pastoral care to be undertaken by specially trained and recognised members of a pastoral team, or leaders of small groups. But this does not remove the problem of the challenge to pastoral equipping. It simply transfers the contract to a different party. The truth is that we need to help people see that when they join a local church, they should expect to be intentionally discipled. In line with God's desire that we grow into maturity, he calls us together into a community of fellow believers to be formed as disciples of Jesus. This is the primary calling of the church (Ephesians 4:15–16). It is true that we have a responsibility to care for one another, but the New Testament call is that this should be 'one to another'. Our primary need is not for professional, paid pastoral care. Instead, we need strong networks of care that enable us to keep walking the path of discipleship.

This is the thrust of the teaching about ministry gifts in Ephesians 4:11–13. The gifts given to the church by the ascended Christ are people – people who carry in themselves the gifts and ministries of the Spirit that enable a community of people to engage in *'works of service'* as well as growing into maturity. These ministries need to be varied: apostolic, prophetic, evangelistic, pastoral and teaching, precisely because the works of service are varied and the maturing of disciples of Jesus is complex.

With all that in mind, here are some practical ideas for how to pastor in a way that equips people for all those various places and tasks.

Visit people on their frontlines

Never underestimate the value of visiting someone, whenever possible, not in their home or at a coffee shop, but on their frontline – the place where they regularly spend time with those who don't follow Jesus: their place of work, for example. Doing so conveys a powerful message about the value of what they do there and demonstrates a wider view of the pastoral role.

And it not only encourages our people that their role as a disciple on their frontline really matters – it also helps deepen our understanding of the places and tasks we're equipping people for. Indeed, LICC's own research shows that churches that successfully embed whole-life disciplemaking in their culture over the longer term have leaders who are curious enough to consistently learn about their people's lives.[2]

Don't feel you need to know everything

We don't need to worry that we aren't experts on the details of every single frontline. You may never have worked in parcel delivery, painting and decorating, or as a paediatrician. You may never have cared for an elderly parent or corralled a horde of small children. Indeed, you won't have personally experienced most of the roles most of the people in your church fulfil. But frontlines that appear very different on the surface often have much more in common than we first think. Christians are all called to serve the same God in and through their day-to-day roles and relationships – wisdom for how to glorify him in railway management isn't so radically different from wisdom for how to glorify him as a parent.

At LICC we've found that almost all (perhaps as much as 80%) of the foundational perspectives workers need in order to understand and live out God's purposes for them in their work are exactly the same for everyone else in a congregation. Everyone needs to know that what they do is significant to God, and why – including the housework. Everyone needs to know how they can be fruitful for God in a whole range of ways – and to see the ways they already have been. And everyone, though they may be the only Christian in their workplace, class at school, seminar at uni, team in the rugby club, needs to go into their everyday mission field with ongoing access to the wisdom, support and prayers of God's people.

Ask the right questions

Even when our people are going through the extremes of life, subtle changes in the questions we ask can give us the chance to pastorally equip them. The role of a pastor is to offer love, prayer and care. But our God is also in the business of bringing good from bad. And in part that means teaching and growing us even in these moments of extremity and crisis. So, when appropriate, and with great care not to push someone who doesn't have the emotional bandwidth for any kind of question, I might ask some of the following:

- How can you respond to what's happening?
- Do you sense anything God's doing in this time?
- Is there anything you need so you don't miss this opportunity to grow?
- What can our church do to support you in this situation, so that you can be most fruitful in it?
- Do you sense any lessons for your everyday situations in the future as a result of what you're going through?

To be clear, I'm not recommending these questions for all people and at all times. There are some pastoral needs and some people for whom these questions would be unhelpful. At the same time, a reworded version of any of these questions may be the very thing that helps to bring about spiritual growth from someone's difficult situation.

To sum up, the fundamental role of a church leader is not to be the principal carer (as important as the caring role is), missionary or events manager. Our fundamental role is to ensure that the community is a disciplemaking one, a church that will help its people to grow in maturity and mission.

Pray about it

Lord, help me to pastor well, for those experiencing good days, uncertain days, bad days, average days and every type of day in between.

Help me to pastorally care and to pastorally equip. Amen.

Vital sign 5
Daily conversations

In a nutshell

When it comes to our informal daily conversations, the best church leaders have a curiosity about their people's everyday lives. They're genuinely interested in the way discipleship plays out in ordinary, daily contexts. This interest and curiosity is vital, because 'gathered' church activities tend to shout for attention, whereas 'scattered' mission whispers.

This chapter focuses on informal conversations rather than planned time as part of a pastoral role. Of course, for some of us as church leaders, the distinction between planned pastoral time and informal conversations is blurred. In fact, it should be blurred – like when the conversation at an evening meal with church friends turns to an unexpected personal issue. But it's helpful to consider informal daily conversations separately. The spontaneous nature of these chats, emails and texts means they so often get missed out in our thinking about equipping people for whole-life discipleship.

LICC's research shows that churches that maintain an emphasis on whole-life discipleship over the long term have leaders who are consistently learning about their people's frontlines. As the 'Sustaining Change' report summarises:

> A hallmark of all the leaders we interviewed is they consciously and consistently take time to learn about what is happening in people's everyday lives. They are genuinely interested in who people are, what they get up to, the challenges they face, the ways they are being fruitful. There is no sense in which they

are just looking for sermon illustrations; they really do care about people and want to learn about their lives.[1]

As we've seen, people in our churches rarely call us about non-extreme things going on in their everyday situations. But they will call, email or WhatsApp about something to do with church life – about a rota, for example. It then requires an act of the will for us as church leaders to say, 'Great – we've covered your question about the rota. But while I've got you, I wanted to let you know I'm praying for you on your frontline. Can you give me one thing to pray about for you today? It doesn't have to be big – I'd love to know what's going on so I can pray for you more meaningfully.'

Our days are full of these informal connections. Depending on the size of your congregation and the population of your village, town or city, you may also bump into your people at all sorts of convenient (and inconvenient!) places and times. Some of these informal opportunities also happen when they come into the church building, if you have one, to set up for an event in the church programme. And, more than for any other generation of church leaders, our people call us and message us while actually on their frontlines.

For me, the hardest element in making the most of these moments is the act of the will. It's not that I lack the required curiosity. It's that busyness can kill the curious questions. I nevertheless need to pause from my busyness and theirs and ask about other things going on in their lives. The good intent is there, but the pressure to move on and press on with my to-do list is significant. Sometimes, of course, it's fine just to talk about the rota. But the opportunities to go beyond the church programme to the frontline issues are more frequent than we think – and we can set the norm. As church leaders, we can take the conversation in a whole-life direction. And if we've established patterns of daily, whole-life-focused prayer and Bible reading (see *Vital sign 1* and *Vital sign 2*), it's much more likely that we'll be ready, willing and praying for these opportunities. To that end, it's worth having some questions up our sleeves to use when the chance arises. For example:

- What are the opportunities and challenges you're facing on your frontline today?
- What's coming up today that I can pray for?

My approach need not be your approach. But most of us will benefit from having some typical questions on hand that show we care and that feel right coming out of our mouths or via email. What might yours be? As one church leader in our research put it: 'Asking good questions is important. Listen well and show people physically that you are listening well, and you just learn stuff. You have to be in it for the long haul and gain people's trust.'[2]

These questions do much more than extract answers for our prayers, though that is vital. They say something about what the church and church leaders value. They help to break down the sacred–secular divide: the implicit belief that God cares more about 'holy' stuff (church services, prayer meetings, charity work and so on) than everything else (jobs, hobbies, concerts, nights out, time with friends). And for the church leader asking the questions, the answers can inform, surprise and encourage.

Here's an example. When one pastor in Staffordshire started making these conversations a habit, she was surprised by just how varied the stories and insights she gained were. There were dramatic stories that might never have been shared, including a taxi driver in the church who had shown kindness to a particular passenger. Years later, the driver had learned that that simple act had moved the passenger from their resolve to take their own life that evening. There was also a factory worker whose daily discipleship challenge was being thoroughly bored at work. Once the pastor discovered these things, she could both reimagine the power of kindness for her people's frontlines and talk and pray about what God's purpose might be in even the most repetitive and unimaginative tasks. These insights might not have come to light without asking the right questions in general conversations.

For me personally, these chats have often led to hearing news before a person might consider it important enough to share. For example, hearing that someone was looking for a change of career helped me to pray both for God's guidance and that they would discover more of God's role for them while they were still in their current role. Whether we're enjoying our current frontline or not, for now we are where we are, and God can work through us there.

The writer and speaker Frederick Buechner offers a helpful perspective:

> If I were called upon to state in a few words the essence of everything I was trying to say both as a novelist and as a preacher, it would be something like this: Listen to your life. See it for the fathomless mystery that it is. In the boredom and pain of it no less than in the excitement and gladness: touch, taste, smell your way to the holy and hidden heart of it because in the last analysis all moments are key moments, and life itself is grace.[3]

In other words, asking someone questions does more than inform us. It's also a key way to invite people to listen to their own lives and to bring this listening to the Lord in prayer, discovering his presence in the midst of their everyday situations. So many people will acknowledge how God is at work in their daily lives more when they're invited to articulate it.

Most of the time, hearing about people's challenges, opportunities and victories on their frontlines greatly encourages me as a church leader and helps strengthen my resolve to keep going with emphasising whole-life discipleship. One of the challenges we often face is that much of the fruit produced by whole-life disciplemaking is out of the church leader's sight. It takes a bit of intentional work to find out about how people are putting their faith into action out in the world, but if we make that effort, the things we discover are so worth it. Indeed, hearing the encouraging stories that crop up in daily conversations is part of what it means to answer Paul's challenge in Philippians 4:8: *'Finally, brothers and sisters, whatever is true, whatever is noble, whatever is right, whatever is pure, whatever is lovely, whatever is admirable – if anything is excellent or praiseworthy – think about such things.'*

The six 'whatevers' and the additional 'if anything' here can be read as a reminder to find good news stories in every part of life, seeing the wonder of what God is doing in and beyond our church programme. Paying attention to good news stories from other people's frontlines is most certainly part of that.

Finally, to listen well during daily conversations is to be reminded of the current reality people are facing in their lives. The experiences one person shares will often apply to many other people in the church. And it's essential we acknowledge this and equip people for those experiences in the nitty gritty of daily life, just as much as for the good times and the gathered-church times.

As church leaders, we spend a lot of time helping to cultivate beautiful places of encounter with God; something close to what the Celtic Christians called 'thin places' – where God's presence seems more accessible, where we enjoy a greater degree of awareness of his presence, where perhaps prayer has been invested over many generations, and where heaven and earth seem to touch in a more tangible way.[4] We need these thin places, and we need to visit them often. But we are not called to live there. Of course, not every place is thin in that sense. Therefore there must be 'thick' places too – places where despite his continued presence, we are less aware of God.

We need to help people remember the lessons learned and the assurances given in the thin places so they can carry them into the thick places. God is the Lord of those places too, and we are called to represent him so well in the thick places that we help make them thinner for those around us.

All this comes back to those informal conversations we have during the week. For the people we chat to, if we push that little bit beyond church business to the stuff of daily life, these conversations can help create a culture in which they feel known not just for the ways they serve in the gathered church, but for who they are and what they do in their everyday lives. As one church member said of their church leader: 'When we get together and talk, we're as likely to talk about my situation at work as we are about church-based ministry. In that sense, it's a better relationship because it's fuller and you're talking about more of your life and you don't feel like you've got to put on the shiny happiness.'[5]

Our informal questions help demonstrate that what our people do outside the church building is just as significant as what they do inside it. And they can confirm that the way we serve society isn't *just* through brilliant church-based activities like debt advice, food banks, and parent and toddler groups, but also through how we serve our customers, bless our neighbours, look out for struggling parents and mould our work culture.

Pray about it

Lord, when unplanned conversations open up, may my questions and my listening speak for you.

May those I chat to know that their frontline is holy, their role is mission, their commute is a pilgrimage, their tools are spiritual, their tasks are ministry and their time is worship. . . Not because of what the job title says, because of the details on the job description or their salary, or even because they love every moment or want to be there. But because they are there with you and for you. Amen.

Section 2

WHEN WE GATHER

Vital sign 6
Sunday gatherings

In a nutshell

A church service should be the opposite of escapism (the tendency to seek distraction and relief from reality). A church service is neither fantasy nor distraction. Our Sunday gatherings offer a chance for recalibration: a reminder of our place in God's purposes for his world, so that when each service ends, we return to our frontlines re-energised, re-equipped and resolved.

I'll admit it. I often watch Netflix purely for entertainment and escapism. When I collapse onto the sofa, I don't want to learn anything (though I often do, regardless). I just want to switch my brain off and passively receive, letting the stress of the day get buried under Scandi drama or high-stakes baking.

But while there is value in a beautifully crafted piece of entertainment and escapism at the end of a long day, we need to be really careful about how much we carry that same attitude into our Sunday meetings. Church is not Netflix for the soul. Everything about our worship services should have a different emphasis. Gathered worship isn't for entertainment. It is for a purpose. That purpose is to glorify God and edify, or build up, his people.

Let's be clear: worship should be engaging, and we certainly don't want our services to be boring. They are vehicles for the message of hope for all of humanity, so if we make them boring, that's a kind of heresy. But the primary aim isn't entertainment. Our focus is factual rather than fictional. We can celebrate the fact that our faith in the living God is incredible while at the same time showing it to be fully credible. We can absolutely welcome those who have doubts and admit our own, but this isn't fiction. In the same way, and most crucially, our purpose is not to distract ourselves from the realities of everyday life. It's to regain God's perspective on that reality. It's recalibration.

My wife Sue has a PhD in chemistry, specifically in the field of self-stratifying paint and surface coatings. In her work, recalibration is the act of checking and adjusting an instrument's action, making sure it hasn't deviated from the original maker's settings. In a lab, recalibration should be prioritised in the diary, occur regularly in a safe place free from interference, and be made against a reliable standard known as a 'master'. I'm sure you can see where I'm going with this: it's a powerful illustration of what our Sunday gatherings are designed to be. Our weekly services are a key part of regularly recalibrating back to our Master's settings. Crucially, we recalibrate to remind ourselves of the gospel in its fullest sense, of all that the good news of Jesus means to us and to the world. And we recalibrate in order to be fit for the purposes God has for us in all of our lives.

No single element of our gathered worship services can be expected do this in isolation. We need to consider all the different elements in our Sunday worship together. Each church will have its own style and norms, and not all the elements I've listed here will apply to your normal patterns, but these are some key things to aim for.

Preaching that equips us for our whole lives

Sermons are like a half-time team talk: an opportunity for the 'players' to be encouraged and refreshed and gain tactical insight that will help them be more effective back on the field of play – in this case, their frontlines. So, at their best, they are part of our forming as disciples who join in the mission of God throughout the week. And those involved in preaching should be 'player-managers' actively involved in the game too.

Within these sermons, as well as drawing out whole-life implications and applications from the Bible, stories from people's present-day frontlines can be powerful illustrations to fuel the implications of the message for us now. The preacher's player-manager role is emphasised when the stories sometimes include examples from their own frontlines, as we discussed in *Vital sign 3*, but being able to share a variety of frontline stories and contexts is equally important. Where relevant, offering a biblical perspective on things going on in contemporary culture – whether films, books, TV shows or news events – can also provide a vital illustration of our faith's whole-life relevance.

Sung worship that points outwards to the places God sends us in the week

Our sung worship should first point us upwards to God and should also help us focus inwards to one another as we gather. But we so often miss the way it can help us look outwards, towards our frontlines. When we do consider that 'outwards' dimension, we shouldn't just be thinking of unknown faces in far-off mission fields, but also of the very familiar places and faces on our frontlines, including our friends and family. For example, it's good to regularly pick songs with lyrics that encourage us to live out the 6Ms of fruitfulness (see page 8) in our daily lives: modelling godly character, making good work, ministering grace and love, moulding culture, being a mouthpiece for truth and justice, and being a messenger of the gospel.

Communion that has a sending aspect

This reminds us that the purpose of our gathering is to be released back out to our frontlines. Our wording or liturgy for the Lord's Supper may already contain this element, but do we draw attention to it? The words at the end of the Anglican Communion often say, 'Send us out in the power of your Spirit to live and work to your praise and glory.' How can we incorporate that message in the way we conduct Communion?

Prayers that include thanking, asking and listening on themes relevant to our frontlines

Prayers for frontline issues, for our role as Christ's ambassadors, as salt and light, need their place alongside the wide variety of themes and topics we pray about when together. While we pray for the global and national headline issues, key events in the gathered-church programme – mission projects we support in the UK and overseas, people with particular needs and sickness, and more – we can look for ways to include prayers for us all as the scattered church in the week ahead.

Notices that mention people's everyday contexts

If we pray for the person who's just got a promotion into a position of influence, or the person who's begun a new chapter as a carer for a relative, or the person who's started a new business venture, it communicates to the congregation that these aspects of daily life matter to God. We notice what gets noticed.

Interviews that spotlight people's everyday mission

For example, you could consider a 'This Time Tomorrow' slot, each week giving a different person the opportunity to share where they'll be on Monday, what opportunities they have to be fruitful there and the challenges they face. Many churches have found these simple stories from their own people to be transformational. Hearing people in your church describe how God has been working on their frontlines, share how they've become aware of the significance of their work, or give thanks for the fruitfulness they've experienced there builds hope and confidence throughout the congregation, including for people with very different frontline situations.

Prayer ministry where people are encouraged to pray for everyday opportunities and challenges, as well as spiritual issues

Some of us tend to feel that an issue has to have a certain level of importance to warrant asking for prayer. It can be very powerful to sometimes simply encourage people to come for prayer support for their everyday frontline situations in the week ahead.

It would be easy to read this list and get the impression that all these elements must have a whole-life emphasis every time we gather. But that would set too high a bar. Every church I've been part of or visited would fail to meet this standard. Not every element in a service needs to be focused on the scattered life of church every time. For example, a song about internal fellowship and love, or an intercession for the sick within our community, or a focused prayer time for our missionaries overseas are all still important elements. In fact, if we were suggesting that every element of every service should always have an explicit whole-life discipleship emphasis, they would each need their own individual chapter in this book.

A wiser approach would be to ask ourselves the following questions to check where our services are at as a whole:

- Does each Sunday gathering have some clear aspects of whole-life encouraging and equipping in the mix?
- Have we made sure none of the service elements undermine the goal of growing whole-life disciples or reinforce the sacred–secular divide we're trying to remove?
- Do we see a whole-life emphasis in all the elements in the service over time, so that it is not always carried by the same element?

As a general rule, the whole-life discipleship message is probably being watered down if it is:

- prayed for but never present in the examples given in the sermon;
- often mentioned in a sermon but never sung about;
- sung about but never newsworthy enough to be included in the notices;
- featured in a 'This Time Tomorrow' slot, but with no relation to the rest of the service.

In one church, the worship leader decided to give a fresh perspective to many of the songs that were frequently sung, thinking specifically of people's frontlines. Without changing any of the lyrics of the songs, the leader looked for any time a song or hymn used words such as 'here' or 'place' or 'presence' – any words that indicated a location. It was found that these words occur remarkably often. While the songwriter probably used 'here' to mean the place of gathered worship, this worship leader encouraged the congregation to also sing the words while picturing their frontlines. The power of singing, 'Build your kingdom here', or, 'We bow down and confess you are Lord in this place,' while reflecting on their everyday places was profound.

When we think about gathering and meeting together, these verses in Hebrews are often quoted: *And let us consider how we may spur one another on towards love and good deeds, not giving up meeting together, as some are in the habit of doing, but encouraging one another – and all the more as you see the Day approaching'* (Hebrews 10:24–25). The word used here for *'meeting together'* implies more than meeting socially. It's the kind of word used for official assembly meetings, so it particularly fits our consideration of the Sunday gathering. More importantly, the message conveyed here is found in far more than just this one isolated passage. We don't just have this one instruction to meet together and not lose the habit; we also see patterns of meeting together all through the New Testament. This is how the disciples learn. It is how the New Testament church letters are first listened to by their original recipients and, crucially, we see the assumption of regularly meeting together throughout the Bible. That's why John Wesley could say, 'The Bible knows nothing of solitary religion.'[1]

And yet these verses in Hebrews are written about the danger of losing this essential pattern. So it's probably worth reminding ourselves why we gather. What are we meeting for? We are meeting because:

- there is the instruction, assumption and pattern in the Bible to do so;
- when we do, we can bring glory to God and build one another up;
- there is a special spiritual significance to being an interdependent group together: all one body playing different parts;
- the call to Christian community is not about what's in it for us individually, but about how others might need us;
- it allows us to spur one another on and encourage one another for the opportunities and challenges we face in our scattered places;
- it's an opportunity to recalibrate – to get back a godly perspective when so much else in our life does the opposite;
- our meeting is more than the sum of the parts. We sense something of the presence of the Spirit and so, in gathering together, we are renewed and revived for whatever lies ahead of us in the rest of the week.

Ultimately, even in verses like these that speak about the importance of our gathered times, it requires some serious mental gymnastics to read the instructions they contain as being aimed solely at what we do when we are together. Our gathered times exist to equip us for our scattered times – in thousands of different frontline contexts. We meet to practise being Christ-like in order to be better at it wherever we find ourselves throughout the week.

Pray about it

Lord, help us to have a beautiful interplay between our gathered and scattered times as a church. May our gathered times equip us for our scattered times and our scattered times help inform what happens in our gathered times.

Help our Sunday worship to be a place where we spur one another on towards love and good deeds. May that love and those good deeds be seen and demonstrated on our frontlines. Amen.

Vital sign 7
Prayer meetings and small groups

In a nutshell

Whenever church groups meet up during the week, there's the opportunity for our whole-life discipleship journey to be encouraged. But unless we're intentional, there's also the ever-present danger that the value of whole-life discipleship might be diminished.

It's clearly easier for each person to have the opportunity to speak and be heard in a smaller group setting. This means a church's regular midweek groups are vital tools for discipleship. What gets shared, prayed for, encouraged and supported in these groups communicates much about the overall priorities of the church, and will either regularly include whole-life discipleship issues or (often unintentionally) exclude them.

All churches have different rhythms and patterns for midweek gatherings, and give these gatherings different names, formats and purposes. But whatever we call them, the lessons are the same. In this chapter, we'll consider two of the most common examples of midweek gatherings: prayer meetings and small groups.

Prayer meetings

When churches gather specifically for prayer it's so easy, in the themes we focus on, to inadvertently but completely skip over the whole subject of being a disciple out in God's world. Frontline issues – the pressures of the NHS secretary's job, the deepening chats over the garden fence, the construction worker's excellent bricklaying – are very rarely church headline issues. As a result, they are unlikely to be the main topic of prayer, and that's a real loss. Imagine the impact it would have, both within and outside the church, if these prayer meetings included focused prayer for specific people's frontlines – for all the ways God is working through his people in their daily lives. Happily, making it happen isn't rocket science. With a bit of conscious effort, this kind of frontline-focused prayer can easily be included.

- When we pray for the missionaries linked to the church, can we frame those prayers within the context of the fact that we're all missionaries in our everyday places?
- When we pray for a particular move of God at upcoming gathered-church events, can we pray for a powerful move of God 'out there', when we're scattered too?
- When we pray for revival, can we pray, 'Start with me'? If so, do we mean start with me in *all* of my life, including my frontlines?
- When we pray about the national and global justice issues of our day, can we also pray we will each be a mouthpiece of truth and justice in the issues we face tomorrow?
- When we pray for peace, can we pray we will each be people of peace in our own spheres of influence?
- When we seek to discern God's guidance for our church, can we include our role as the church of God in our everyday places?
- When we pray for our government and royal family, can we pray for our bosses and those in our churches with management responsibility for others?

On that last point, we often quote 1 Timothy 2:1–2: *'I urge, then, first of all, that petitions, prayers, intercession and thanksgiving be made for all people – for kings and all those in authority, that we may live peaceful and quiet lives in all godliness and holiness.'* But it's important to note that the instruction to pray for kings and those in authority is not given in isolation. It is surrounded by a wider whole-life context. While it is important to pray for those in authority, the preceding instruction is to offer prayers, intercessions and thanksgiving for *all people*. Also, *all those in authority* is a wide enough term to include those in our church communities who hold senior positions in their daily lives, whether paid or voluntary. And lastly, these prayers have the brilliant whole-life aim *that we may live peaceful and quiet lives in all godliness and holiness*.

As we consider the list of prayer topics above, it would be too simplistic to say that every time we mention topic X, we should immediately balance it with frontline counterpoint Y. That clearly isn't realistic or appropriate. But the greater danger is that we rarely include everyday frontline issues because there is an unspoken understanding that this isn't what our prayer times together are for. And that would be a great shame.

Small groups

There are many different names for small groups: house groups, home groups, life groups, cell groups, connect groups, growth groups and more. Sometimes the different names imply slightly different things, and sometimes two churches will use exactly the same name and mean slightly different things! They generally have enough in common for us to apply some common lessons, however.

All these small groups provide an excellent environment for our growth as disciples. Lots of them include three basic elements: the Bible, prayer and care, with different amounts of time given to each, depending on the group. At their best, these elements provide the perfect context to consider our frontlines and our whole-life discipleship. There is the potential in a small group to share what's going on in our lives, apply what we're learning in the Bible to these everyday situations, and pray into our various frontlines until we next meet up. As one small group leader put it: 'We get stuck into the Bible, learn what it says, connect it to our lives. We are called to live like Jesus among ordinary people in everyday life. If we're not helping one another to do that when we meet, what's the point?'[1]

One independent evangelical church in Devon has the pattern of providing small-group questions in the weekly news sheet related to the main Sunday sermon. They make sure at least one question is frontline focused, asking people to contextualise the implications and applications from their sermon to their own frontlines.

In many ways, there's nothing radical about this concept, but that doesn't mean it comes naturally. For instance, some small groups may want to 'just' support one another, and they feel that discussing whole-life discipleship doesn't fit in with that goal, perhaps because it feels too 'pressured'. But this raises a question: if we're supporting one another, what are we supporting one another *for*? Surely part of the answer is that by supporting one another we not only provide therapeutic encouragement (which is important), but also help one another to keep growing as disciples through life's ups and downs.

This is just one example. Whatever the situation, three common factors often lead to letting the whole-life focus drift away in small groups. First, in our efforts to look at Bible passages in depth, we sometimes forget to make the connection with our ordinary lives (see *Vital sign 2* for more on this). Someone – often the person leading the session – has to be brave enough to stop and ask, 'So what? What does this passage mean for us right now? What are the implications and applications for your context and mine tomorrow?'

Second, it's all too easy for small-group 'sharing' to have an unspoken hierarchy. The question 'Does anyone have anything they'd like prayer for?' can so easily come to mean 'Does anyone have anything *particularly significant* they'd like prayer for?' Of course, no one actually says that, but it's implied. And when this culture develops, there's a real danger that our everyday kingdom opportunities go unspoken and unshared. At its worst, it feels like a game of Top Trumps. Unless my prayer request hits the unspoken threshold of seriousness or spiritual importance, I won't share it.

Of course, sometimes there is something so major going on for one member of the group that it should rightly dominate. That's a big part of what small groups are for. We're brothers and sisters in Christ, and gathering around to pray is, of course, what a family does in those circumstances. But not every week should be like that. With this in mind, any of the following questions can help draw out more everyday sharing and conversation:

- What opportunities do you currently have to make a difference on your frontline?
- What is a current pressure point for you there?
- What might God's purpose be for you there right now?

Additionally, small-group leaders can set an example by sharing something for prayer from their own frontline.

Third, we can neglect the fact that our care for one another may sometimes include challenging one another. If I really care for those in my small group and if they really care for me, then a certain degree of honesty and openness needs to be involved. Sometimes, this might mean that the loving response is more than empathy and a place of support when we've done the wrong thing. We do need that, but we also need the challenge to prayerfully get back on track. At their best, small groups become a space where, centred together around the Bible and in the power of the Holy Spirit, we find wisdom for how best to seek first God's kingdom, starting with our everyday contexts.

When all's said and done, small groups that maintain a whole-life emphasis increasingly know one another as whole people, not just as 'church-life' people. The support they show for one another naturally spills out beyond their time in someone's home. The Bible, prayer and care continue in the week. It can feel much lonelier and more vulnerable to be a Christian on our frontlines than in gathered-church settings, and we are not meant to go it alone. We have the promise of God being with us by his Spirit, and far more than any other generation of Christians, we have the ability to be with one another remotely during the week. We can message one another reminders of relevant verses we've discussed in our group, or send an assurance of prayer or simply a caring message. If I know my small group have my back and are praying for me, my confidence grows. If I know they will ask me how the challenging opportunity went next time we meet, my resolve grows too.

The sum of all these suggested changes often requires a change of norms and habits for a small group. For some, it will be quite a big shift, while for others, including new people joining in, it will seem like the most natural thing ('How could a small group be about anything else?'). Whichever end of the scale your group is on, it's worth regularly reminding one another of the intention, and checking that the whole-life focus hasn't drifted. We can regularly say something like, 'Let's be intentional about using our Bible study, prayer and sharing to support one another for our everyday mission.' Sometimes, at the of end our session, let's ask one another if we've kept true to that aim.

Small groups are often strongly independent and develop their own style. This isn't just inevitable; it is healthy. Within every style, though, there is room to emphasise whole-life discipleship, and this may take deliberate and consistent encouragement. It is also very possible that one or two groups will be ahead of the church when it comes to whole-life discipleship. This may have been their natural emphasis for many years, even before the church centrally committed to it. Wherever this is discovered, of course it is a wonderful encouragement and answer to prayer. Our Lord has gone ahead of us, and there may well be lessons from this small group for the others in the church.

Pray about it

Lord, we recognise the vital role our prayer meetings and small groups play in our church. Thank you for them. We're also so thankful for those who lead and take part. Help us to help them embed whole-life discipleship in their thinking and practice.

Lord, show us if we drift back to emphasising gathered-church activities and national and global issues at the expense of our people's everyday challenges and opportunities. Help us to find a healthy mix. Amen.

Vital sign 8
Age- and stage-focused work

In a nutshell

Making the whole-life vision real in work at every age and stage shows that we're seeking to integrate discipleship into every area of our congregation's life. No one is left out of the amazing call to live wholeheartedly for Christ. No one is too young, too old or too busy for God to work through them, right where they are.

In this chapter, we'll use the terms 'age and stage work' and 'age and stage group' as catch-alls for any church activity that focuses on particular age groups or stages of life – think kids' work, youth work, young adult ministries, groups for workers, groups for parents and toddlers, right the way through to groups for retirees. Two additional things are worth noting. First, if you are considering people who are moving from one age or stage to another, take a look also at *Vital sign 17*, which considers times of transition. Second, don't worry if your church consists almost exclusively of one age group. The lessons of this chapter apply just as much to 'accidental' age-focused groups as to intentional ones. And indeed, even in mixed-age churches, sometimes a particular group ends up being age- or stage-focused organically rather than by design.

A whole-life focus in these groups is vital. It is possible for church leaders to be fully committed to whole-life discipleship in their main gatherings and events, yet not see this flow into these age and stage groups. There are many reasons for this. Sometimes we have great voluntary leaders overseeing these groups who themselves have inherited a sacred–secular-divided way of thinking. Sometimes these great people are busy volunteering in their groups while the key aspects of the whole-life message are being taught to the rest of the church – particularly if they run the Sunday kids' groups. Or perhaps they can speak positively about 'whole-life discipleship', but behind that term, their picture of all it entails is limited.

As a result, one church leader might be busy explaining the value of the 6Ms of fruitfulness (see the 'Key terms in this book' section on page 8 for more on those), while at the same time the teaching in one of the age and stage groups is that our work 'out there' is only about the sixth 'M' – being a messenger of the gospel. And in all of this, at each age and stage it's very easy to fill people's diaries with gathered-church activities at the expense of their frontline calling.

The sacred–secular divide can drift back into our churches through any of our age and stage groups. The stories told and the examples given within them are just as influential as those in a Sunday sermon. The retirees' group, for example, may be focused more on fellowship than on purpose, leaving people feeling as though they're too old to have a frontline mission. Or at the other end of the scale, youth work may focus heavily on encouraging teenagers to take gap years 'for God', with little reference to the opportunities they'd have to serve him in vocational or study-based years out. But if there is a danger of whole-life discipleship declining in these groups, there is also a major opportunity for growth. Age and stage groups can be stumbling blocks for whole-life discipleship, but at their best, they can be vital building blocks.

In Deuteronomy 6:6–7, after Moses delivers the Ten Commandments to the people, he picks out the importance of the youngest age group with the instruction to *'impress them on your children'*. But the verses also make it clear that we all need reminders of the key lessons in following God at every stage of life: *'These commandments that I give you today are to be on your hearts. Impress them on your children. Talk about them when you sit at home and when you walk along the road, when you lie down and when you get up.'* It's vital, then, for senior leaders to spend time with leaders of all ages and stages, to make sure they really get whole-life discipleship.

This is one of the reasons we use the word 'frontline' throughout this book to describe the everyday places where we regularly spend time with people who don't know Jesus. It's a particularly helpful term when it comes to age and stage work, because it applies to all age groups and stages of life. Everyone has a frontline. For many, it will be a workplace. For kids, it will probably be school. For students, a university. For retirees, time with friends or volunteering on boards or pursuing hobbies. For parents, it is often the other parents at the school gates, birthday parties or weekend clubs that become their frontline. At any age and stage of work, it's worth asking whether the stories that get told and celebrated are of pastors, missionaries or other gathered-church roles, or whether they include instances from frontlines like the ones listed above, including examples from that particular group's age and stage. In other words, do the retirees only hear about 30-somethings on overseas mission, or do they hear about fellow 70-somethings making a massive difference by sharing their expertise in voluntary roles or radically caring for their unchurched grandkids as a family frontline? And so on.

Another point to note is that sometimes these age and stage groups can be seen purely as places of connection and support. While this is a beautiful aspect of church family life that should rightly be pursued, our challenge is to widen the aims of these groups to include equipping people to grow more fruitful. In practice, that means asking, 'What does being a Christian look like for those in this group when they're not in church? Have we helped them to imagine Jesus living their life?'

A simple way of answering that question is to look at how the 6Ms of fruitfulness (see page 8) apply specifically to this age or stage. What might it look like for our youth or students or parents or retirees to model godly character, make good work, minister grace and love, mould culture, be mouthpieces for truth and justice and be messengers of the gospel? Each season of life, from antenatal classes to school gates to university lectures to paid work to retirement, can provide new frontlines with new opportunities and challenges. If our groups keep these questions to the fore and review their sessions in the light of them, it will provide a helpful reminder and checklist.

To see how these principles can be applied in our own churches, let's work through four examples of groups.

Groups for those in school

If we're leading groups for school-age kids, are we helping them to consider how they can approach their study and activities with God and for God? We might do this by explaining God's promise to be with us always, our commitment to serve him, and how that might play out at school – perhaps in the way they treat others in the playground, or the effort they put into their homework, or how they speak to teachers.

Similarly, are we helping them to think through how their school subjects matter to God? We might do this by pointing out that our creative, wise God has given us creativity and wisdom too, and invites us to join in his work in the world as his image-bearers. Our God is the inventor of both aesthetic beauty and mathematical complexity, and he surely cheers on every creative act and problem-solving move we make.

Finally, have we countered the idea that the greatest path a young person can pursue is a journey into theological education, church or parachurch ministry, or overseas aid and missionary activity? We can do this by underlining that the greatest path a young person can take is to follow Jesus in whatever area of study, work or activity he calls them into.

Groups for young adults

Barna's research[1] highlights some of the reasons why many young adults are leaving the church. Mostly they're not running away because they don't believe. It seems they're drifting away because they don't see the relevance of Christian faith to the questions they wrestle with in their daily lives. The whole-life discipleship vision is exactly what's needed to show that relevance.

LICC has found that whether we have this age group in our churches or not, looking at the questions they're asking focuses our minds and prayers on subjects that are relevant for so many of us. Among many whole-life questions, we've found five come to the fore for 18–35s:

1 How do I share my faith without losing my friends?
2 How do I find purpose in my actual work?
3 How can I establish healthy rhythms in my life?
4 How do I stay human in an inhuman system?
5 How can I make connections with and learn from mentors and peers?

If these are the key questions, let's seek to regularly address them. One church that attracts a large number of students in a university town attempts to do something very much along these lines. It considers the specific Sundays that students may be present over three years. It lists the key discipleship lessons it would hope for them to have received before they leave university and it then makes sure these key lessons are repeated in the term-time weeks over the three years. This could be in age-related small groups or in Sunday services.

Groups for parents

Every stage of parenting throws up its own discipleship opportunities and challenges. Consider the common frontline of the primary-school gate, dropping off and picking up kids. There are 190 school days a year. From Reception to Year 6, that's 1,330 days. If you're spending an average of ten minutes with other parents and carers at the start and end of each day, that's 443 hours. During these seven years, a whole range of life opportunities and challenges will occur for you and others. And that's without having a second child or more attending the same school! These are the kinds of moments we can share and pray about when parents gather, asking God to work through those interactions and conversations.

Groups for retirees

Then there are groups for those of retirement age. It's not unusual for churches that start focusing on whole-life discipleship to hear a tone of regret from this group – something along the lines of, 'If only I'd heard about this before, when I was in work, I could have applied it. But those days are gone.' The challenge here is for retiree groups to point out that the opportunities may have changed in later life, but they absolutely remain. Older people's frontlines may include continuing to offer work expertise in voluntary roles, deliberately joining social groups outside of the church, as well as time with neighbours, friends and family. Sometimes there is an additional challenge associated with rediscovering a sense of identity and purpose that had previously been linked to work and status. My own church was brilliantly served by people in the early years of retirement serving in multiple church activities, but I always hoped that time spent in and for the church didn't come at the expense of the frontlines they could form.

It's worth all of us taking stock. Every age and stage in church life provides an opportunity to reinforce the whole-life message, but also the danger of undermining it. Are there any ages and stages in your church that need particular attention and encouragement to emphasise whole-life discipleship?

Pray about it

Lord, for each age and stage group in my church, I pray that those attending would know that you're with them on their frontlines this week and that Jesus is Lord there, whatever happens. I pray for eyes to see where they are already being fruitful on their frontlines.

Lord, grow their vision and mine of what living for Jesus might look like where they are. Across the generations, may we encourage and support one another for our own ages and stages. Amen.

Vital sign 9
Annual festivals and seasons

In a nutshell

When it comes to the big seasons in the church year – Easter, Christmas, Remembrance Sunday and so on – the calendar can be full to bursting and we hope our buildings will be too. But as church leaders, it's all too easy to think of these seasons purely in terms of what's happening in the gathered church, rather than considering the way they're worked out in our people's everyday frontline contexts.

When it comes to annual Christian festivals, some of us have more than others! Almost all our churches will have a programme of some sort for Christmas and Easter. Most will have some sense of Advent in the run-up to Christmas and may well include something for Lent in the run-up to Easter. Many will consider Pentecost a significant event or hold a Harvest Festival or a Plough Sunday. Some churches celebrate a saint's day connected with their church (a 'patronal day'), or their church's anniversary. The list goes on – your church probably marks a few annual days I've not mentioned here!

Whatever festivals and seasons you celebrate, the chances are each one brings plenty of admin and forward planning with it – getting the right decorations, planning the activities for the kids, arranging special slots in the service. These are all good things that rightly need our attention. But what if, in addition to focusing on the opportunities and challenges that happen inside the church building, we also prayerfully considered the particular frontline opportunities and challenges each season brings? When the mind is so full of Christmas or Easter planning, it can be very tempting to think, 'I'll get back to emphasising whole-life discipleship when this is over.' But if we drop the frontline emphasis in this season, just until we get back to more normal days, what does that say? We will have diminished the value of whole-life discipleship, making it something to talk about when other, more important, things aren't happening.

The point here is that this isn't an either/or situation. It's possible to give our gathered events at these festivals and seasons high priority while not forgetting the parallel frontline opportunities and challenges for our people.

For a start, most of us are aware that these special seasons are a great opportunity for people to offer invitations to the people on their frontlines. Invitations to a church service or event are a good thing! And the special services around these festival occasions are often the times when an invitation seems most natural. Sometimes we need to remind, encourage and even embolden our people to give good invitations to their frontline friends, family and colleagues. Most new people who come to these seasonal services do so as the result of a well-made invitation, and more people say yes than we might think. It's really important we encourage folk not to say someone else's 'no' for them by pre-deciding they'll decline the invitation so it's not worth asking them in the first place.

In my own church, I can name a number of people who first attended at Christmas or Easter and then joined an Alpha course before ultimately finding faith in Jesus and a spiritual home in our church. It doesn't always happen – I can also think of some who ended up finding a spiritual home in another church because they lived too far away to come regularly to our church – but it is a significant thing when our frontline friends come to our gathered-church events, and you never know where that will lead. After all, the Bible readings during all these seasons are full of whole-life themes and messages. The traditional Christmas readings, for example, celebrate God stepping into a particular time and place, complete with multiple everyday situations – workplaces, political issues, travel arrangements, dilemmas and decisions. The good news is placed in a manger, not a palace or temple. Outsiders are invited from their everyday places to join in the story. A whole-life message that includes these elements could be just what a particular guest needs to hear to understand that their ordinary life matters to God.

With all that said, though, there's a big caveat we should bear in mind when encouraging invitations, because the reality is that most people's frontline friends might never walk into a church building, even during a special festival or season. When I pause and pray about this reality, it helps me reframe my priorities.

Let's carry on with Christmas as an example, because it's the season and festival that almost all of our churches feature strongly in more than one service. To do that, let's look at Luke 1, one of the Bible passages most of us will focus on during this period. Consider the contrast between the priest Zechariah's reaction to an angelic visit, and Mary's reaction twenty verses later: *'Zechariah asked the angel, "How can I be sure of this? I am an old man, and my wife is well on in years"* (Luke 1:18) and *"'I am the Lord's servant," Mary answered. "May your word to me be fulfilled"'* (Luke 1:38).

These two characters, described one after the other, were perhaps as shocking to their original audience as the priest Levite and the Samaritan were in Jesus' parable of the Good Samaritan. They would have expected Zechariah the mature priest to be the one full of faith, responding most readily. But instead, it's the everyday young woman, Mary, without any notable status or wealth, who plays this role. She seems to have more faith that God will fulfil his promises than Zechariah does, an official priest and serving member of the clergy. There are many lessons here, but one important thing we can take away is a question: how often do we hear or tell stories in which the hero is not the person with the so-called 'spiritual' job?

Which brings us back to the point I made earlier. Many people won't come to our churches for the key events and sermons we've shaped for them. But they *will* ask the Christians on their frontlines about them. They *will* ask how their weekend was. They *will* ask afterwards if they had a good Christmas.

When I was leading a church, I was very aware that my congregation wouldn't get thirty minutes to explain the miracle of the incarnation to their colleagues in the office. Instead, they'd maybe get thirty seconds to say something to spark the imagination and demonstrate that Christmas was significant to them. After those thirty seconds, it would be back to work, or someone else would enter the room and the conversation would no longer be appropriate – but it might be picked up again at any moment. Have I helped prepare them for this? How can what we do in church equip them to fill those thirty seconds well? When I play golf at my local club, the members know I am a Christian and a minister, they may ask something briefly but then drop the subject when someone else is within ear-shot. They may then pick up that conversation a month later. The discipline of offering short responses in the time allowed has been good for me as a preacher!

We also need to remember that fruitfulness during these seasons isn't just about the words people speak – it's about the way they act. Many non-Christians won't come to our churches at Christmas, but they will go out for coffee or a drink or to the Christmas party with the people from our churches. These next-level social settings bring their own opportunities and challenges. I might be encouraging Jo, who's new in her office, to invite her friends to the nativity service, but in reality her most pressing issues are whether to go to the Christmas party, how much to drink if she does, and how to navigate the heavy cloud of gossip that floats over the whole thing. These are very real whole-life discipleship questions.

So, with all that in mind, and continuing with our Christmas example, what does our planning for this season look like as church leaders? Speaking from my own experience, when I was a leader in a local church this season was *so* busy. The first challenge was to pause long enough to remember and contemplate the miracle of the incarnation afresh myself. There was a genuine danger that I could stand up and speak with a fresh idea and illustration, but without any sense of wonder and gratitude in my own life. I remember vividly one year sitting in a study in the church building, preparing a message for what would be a packed 'carols by candlelight' service. All of a sudden, there was a knock on the door. I opened it and standing outside was – I kid you not – a heavily pregnant young woman and her partner, who had nowhere to stay that night and needed help from the church. I very nearly turned them away so I could prepare the important sermon before I realised the connection and the irony!

The point I'm making is that if you ask a church leader what Christmas means for their role, most will think of the times when we gather in churches. Rightly so, in many ways. But if our planning for Christmas stops there, we'll be neglecting plans to equip people for the places where most of them spend most of their time, mixing with people who wouldn't call themselves Christians. So, let's take a few examples of what it might look like to incorporate people's scattered lives into our gathered activities at Christmas; these principles can just as well be applied to any other annual festival or season.

Suppose Ayanna in your church is a GP. For Ayanna, the run-up to Christmas is full of people carrying the extra tension of wanting to be well for the big day. The time since the peak of the pandemic has been hugely stressful for GPs, with pent-up demand leading to extra anxiety and extra issues to discuss (rather than the regulation 'one per appointment'), and longer waiting lists for many key hospital procedures. Now add to that people coming in early on Christmas Eve wanting an instant, over-the-counter cure for whatever problem they have so they can get on with Christmas. What does it look like to be a Christian GP in those circumstances? There are no easy answers, but we can pray when we are gathered together about the kind of wisdom and love Ayanna is going to need, recognising that she is living out the Christmas message of hope and peace in that stressful environment.

Or imagine you have a friend in your church called Faisal, who runs his own business. Some businesses are at their busiest at Christmas, but Faisal runs a car showroom, and this is one of his quietest seasons. Not many cars are sold in December. And that brings faith challenges and opportunities. In this season with lower sales, there's anxiety for Faisal as he faces all the same outgoings, including higher heating bills, against lower takings. At the same time, the relative lack of customers also means more opportunity for deeper, longer conversations with colleagues. At the other end of the scale, for people in our churches who work in high street retail this is the busiest time. Their colleagues might truly benefit from someone carrying God's greater perspective and peace amid the flood of customer demands, stock-taking and shelf-stacking.

Or consider Pam and Kevin. They're retired, and at some point in the Christmas season they'll have a big family gathering for a couple of days, with children and grandchildren. They've prayed faithfully for all of them, but they don't come to church services. They might come to the Christmas Day service, or they might not. Even if they do, that's only forty-five minutes to an hour. We can pray for the challenges Pam and Kevin will face. All big family gatherings are a loving compromise of timings, taste choices, and volume and heating preferences, aren't they? But there are opportunities too – opportunities to discuss what happened in the service and to convey the love of Jesus in word and deed. Pam and Kevin's church have been praying that those from younger generations might come along to their church events this Christmas. While that might not always have happened, they *have* been walking into their parents' and grandparents' homes and receiving Christ-like hospitality. Pam and Kevin's family receive much of the message of Jesus as they display the fruit of the Spirit in their home.

The chances are your church will be full of examples like this. The teacher just managing to find the energy to keep going to the end of term. The plumber with emergency call-outs from people desperately wanting immediate help. The parent with the pressure to make this season extra special for their kids. The waiter or waitress with so much of their restaurant's income dependent on this season. In your gathered times, how can you encourage and equip them to see those places and tasks as crucial to their Christian ministry – that God has put them there for a reason and is working through them?

We've used Christmas as our primary example here, but there are parallel lessons for each special season or annual festival in the life of our church. As church leaders, while we consider our gathered events and invitation opportunities, let's also challenge ourselves to consider how we can equip people to join in with what God's doing on their scattered frontlines.

Pray about it

Lord, when major seasons and annual events come up, help me to remember that wonderful opportunities happen both when we are gathered together and when we are scattered. May those who walk into our events as guests or find us online get more than they bargained for. May the same be true for those who don't come to our services but do spend time with our people.

Give your people wisdom, care and love to use well the opportunities you give them. Amen.

Vital sign 10
Births, deaths, marriages and baptisms

In a nutshell

Special occasions require special whole-life discipleship consideration. There are so many demands and considerations on these unique occasions in church that discipleship can be missed. But equally, there's a unique opportunity, with a unique audience, to connect these special occasions with the whole lives of the person or people being remembered or celebrated.

When it comes to special services to mark key aspects of people's lives – baptisms, dedications, marriages and funerals in particular – there are some obvious theological differences between different churches and denominations, as well as a wide variety of practice and frequency of occurrence. For some churches, at least one of these special services will occur most weeks. For others, they may happen less than once a year. Whatever we do and however we do it, the truths that unite us as disciples of Jesus are greater than our differences. And whenever these special services occur, there are opportunities to reinforce the whole-life discipleship vision – helping those in attendance recognise that the symbolism in play has relevance for every part of the life they live outside the building.

These special services are also significant because the guests who come often include those who don't normally attend any gathered-church services. As wonderful as that is, it also makes it easy to think something along the lines of, 'Surely this is the time to focus on the gathered event, to concentrate on conveying the message of hope we have in Jesus while our people's friends, family and colleagues are with us.'

Yes – absolutely! But this is also the moment to join in with what God is doing out in his world, and help people make whole-life discipleship connections. Pointing out that the words we speak during ceremonies like these convey a purpose and meaning inherent in all the details of life may be just the message those attending need to hear – and, in fact, they may not have heard it at any other point in their lives. The desire to bring people in to hear the gospel and the desire to send them out that bit more aware of God's call on their whole lives work together well. We don't have to choose one or the other.

Some of these services may be held for people who have no other church connection but come wanting and needing our help on these occasions. If I'm involved in a service like this, I realise that it brings a particular opportunity to serve well and do good work. Of course, I want to give my best during all services, recognising that I am ultimately serving our God. But whenever the majority of attendees have no church connection, I'm particularly aware that my 'doing good work' will be seen by some who'll assess church and the Christian faith in the light of their experience with us. At other times, the service is for someone who is or has been very much a part of the Christian community. If I'm speaking or leading on these occasions, I need to remember that the guests attending include that person's frontline friends and family coming to us. Anything I say or do should logically join in and connect with the whole-life message the guests have already seen in the person they know.

To be honest, I've sometimes found that these busy, important occasions can be a time when my own unconscious sacred–secular divide comes to the surface. For example, I once led a funeral service of a much-loved older man in our church. I'd known this man well. I'd learned a lot from him, loved and respected him, and had served alongside him as a leader in our church. The service was packed to overflowing, and alongside family tributes I was able to speak to family and friends about all he meant to those of us in the church. At the end of the service, I spoke with some of his old work colleagues who were there. They had been very moved by the whole service, but they also wanted to comment on his career. 'You didn't mention what a great administrator he was for the NHS. He was first-rate at his job, a privilege to work with.' I was able to take time then to ask them more and hear some of their stories. Reflecting back, I realised I had known of his NHS career, but I only had first-hand experience of his voluntary service in church. In the service, I expressed what I knew well at the expense of a key frontline and a huge part of his life.

Of course, the way a special service can communicate the whole-life vision will depend on which of the different types of service we're considering. What's appropriate in a wedding service is unlikely to work in a funeral and vice versa. Let's consider the different examples.

Funerals

Funerals often offer the opportunity to hear someone's life story for the first time or in more detail. Jo, in her training as a Church of England curate, was encouraged to make space to hear stories of the life of the person for whom she was taking the funeral – especially when they weren't known by the church previously. It's a real privilege to be asked to step into this important family moment, and the last thing she wanted was to offer a sterile, off-the-peg funeral service. Jo used to make extra time to sit and hear as many stories as she could, encouraging the family to put a sheet of paper on the table and jot down memories as they came up. Whole-life pastoring is about serving the whole person – in this case seeking to listen in a way that served the emotional, spiritual and practical needs of the family.

For one woman, she was given a sheet of stories of 'Nonna': ways in which this lovely Christian Italian woman had cared for her kids, valuing her role as a mother and grandmother. Another woman had been heavily involved in charity work at a local cat shelter, and her love and care for God's creatures was a huge part of her life. Working these whole-life elements into a funeral service was a gift to each of these families,, who felt understood, but it was also a celebration of the way their faith had shaped their whole lives. And as Jo listened to the lives of these women, she was able to write prayers thanking God for the people they were in all the details of their lives. Interestingly, both of them had been Christians, but for years had been housebound. 'Nonna' had relocated to be near her family and spoke little English; the second woman had come to faith over the internet, but had never been well enough to go to church. They weren't on any rotas, weren't well known in the local church, but they were women who trusted in Jesus. Celebrating the way they followed Christ throughout their lives, inside and outside of formal church activities, was important. These moments of stopping and reflecting on their history were beautiful windows into their whole-life discipleship.

Psalm 23 is possibly the most common passage chosen for funerals. Certainly 'The Lord's my Shepherd', which uses the words of this psalm, is among the most popular hymns. It's a wonderful passage, full of appropriate words for the occasion, full of the promise of God's presence in all circumstances, including walking 'through the darkest valley', and pointing to eternity, dwelling 'in the house of the Lord for ever'.

But before this eternal promise, David is assured of God's goodness and love following him 'all the days' of his life. At the heart of this 'funeral' hymn is an everyday promise for our frontlines. And when we read any of David's psalms we can be assured that they come from his whole-life experience as a shepherd or soldier or king. Like David, we can also trust that God's love will follow us in all the detail of our ordinary days:

> Surely your goodness and love will follow me
>   all the days of my life,
> and I will dwell in the house of the Lord
>   for ever.
> (Psalm 23:6)

Births and baptisms

As well as celebrating the life God has given us, christening, dedication and baptism services include opportunities to pray for God's best for the person concerned in their life ahead, committing them to the Lord for the rest of their days. There is room here for the sacred–secular divide to seep in, if we place an emphasis on the roles they may perform in the gathered church. More positively, though, there is also an opportunity for whole-life discipleship to spill out; for there to be words that point to the life that lies ahead of the person, including their vocation – wherever God calls them. We so easily think of vocations purely in terms of church roles, but it's worth remembering that the word comes from the Latin word *vocare*, which simply means 'to call'. Vocation is about all of God's calling, in every part of life. When we baptise people, we baptise them into an active, living faith, into a church family that is tasked with playing its part in the redemption of all things – at work, in school, at home and beyond.

With all that in mind, in our christening, dedication and baptism services perhaps we could pray something like: 'Lord, may this person be a blessing wherever they find themselves in the days and years to come, wherever you call them. May they daily find their vocation with friends, family, colleagues, customers, patients, clients – whoever you put them with. May they represent you well in the work they do, the relationships they grow and the places they go.'

Marriages

In a sense, every wedding sermon is a whole-life message, particularly if the couple are committed Christians. I don't remember hearing a wedding message that emphasised to the couple the importance of their giving to the church or volunteering within it, or even one that spent much time talking about the gathered church at all. Most of the time, wedding messages point outwards to the couple's lives and connections outside of the gathered church. And if the couple have little or no connection with church or faith, then every interaction with them before, during and after the service demonstrates something of our faith. As people who believe in marriage, there is the opportunity in the service for the couple and all those attending to be pointed to the God who wants the best for each of us for the whole of our lives. (All the lessons from *Vital sign 16*, 'When the frontline comes to us', are relevant here too.)

With any of these events, the whole-life aspect of discipleship can also be relevant to and compelling for those who come and aren't yet Christians. First, if the person concerned is or was a Christian, their non-Christian friends and family may realise in a new way the connection between the person whose faith they're celebrating and the life they see or saw that person live. Rather than seeing Adam or Kerry or whoever as just a nice person to work with, they may realise their behaviour, compassion and peace stems or stemmed from their faith. The message we convey in a service may join up the dots for those present, connecting the everyday spoken and unspoken messages shared by their friend when with them.

Secondly, the message that all work, paid and unpaid, matters to God can be transformational. It points to the possibility of purpose in life and may be one of the key missing elements people need to help them find faith.

Very often, throughout any of these special services, I'm praying that we serve everyone well. I'm also praying that those who attend get more than they expected. While we conduct a service with as much care and craft as possible, we hope they also discover something new about the God who is Lord of all; that the God of the church they are attending for this one day is the God who wants the best for them tomorrow and cares about every place they will find themselves in.

Pray about it

Lord, on these days full of joy or sorrow, our to-do list and our minds can be full too. Help us not to miss the whole-life edge to these special services we're involved in.

In the official parts of the service and the informal chats, please lead and guide our words. May our words point to the God whose goodness and love is with us 'all the days' of our lives. Amen.

Section 3

WHEN WE PLAN

Vital sign 11
Leaders' meetings

In a nutshell

Whole-life discipleship is not good at competing for attention. It needs champions in leaders' meetings to regularly remind us of its importance and bring a whole-life discipleship perspective to the activities, initiatives and teaching being considered.

The points raised in this chapter may particularly apply to an overall church leadership team, but they're also absolutely relevant for teams that lead specific aspects or ministries in the church, like sung worship, small groups, prayer ministry or community work.

PCCs, deacons, elders, plain old 'leaders' . . . every church stream has its own term for the group of people who have overall oversight responsibilities, and even churches that share the same word can have different approaches to leading and gathering as leaders. The ways in which churches are structured as charities also varies, as does the overlap between trustees and other leaders. And in some churches, people don't want to use the word 'leadership' at all for what should be seen as a serving role! Confused yet? Whatever you call it and however it works in your church, don't skip this vital sign if I've not used your preferred term. For this chapter, we'll use 'leadership team' as the best available catch-all phrase.

So, with that housekeeping done, picture a group in your church whose role is to meet and pray about, discern and discuss the key issues in the life of the church. To what extent does that meeting aim to embed whole-life disciplemaking in the culture of the church? As a reminder, that means shaping the things we do in a way that equips and inspires people to join in with what God's doing in their

Monday to Saturday lives, as well as what he's doing on Sunday. If your truthful answer is, 'We always prioritise embedding whole-life discipleship in all aspects of all our meetings,' then on behalf of the rest of us church leaders I offer many congratulations. You win! Collect £200 and move to the next chapter.

The reality for most of us is that many things compete for time and attention in leaders' gatherings. Meetings about the key issues *in the life of* the church can so easily become meetings about the key issues *of life in* the church. In that small grammatical change, whole-life discipleship can be lost. When we're discussing the life *of* the church, there's room to remember that we remain the church when we are scattered on our frontlines, seeking to serve God well in a variety of places. But when we more exclusively discuss life *in* the church, it so easily becomes a discussion solely about our programme for gathered church and the headline pastoral issues our people are facing. These are both vitally important, but as we've seen throughout this book, they're not the only things with which we're tasked. Of course, dominant issues dominate leaders' meetings, and of course pastoral matters matter. But leaders' meetings shouldn't just be controlled by what's urgent – they should also be shaped by what's important.

If we can agree from the start that our people's everyday contexts are an important aspect of our church, then we need to find creative ways to include them in our leadership meetings. This challenge requires an innovative approach, because most leadership teams have no problem filling their meetings, and the norms of our times together can be fairly well set. Words can take time away from thoughtful silence. Discussion can take time away from prayer. The urgent can take all the time away from the important. Our commitment to whole-life discipleship will suffer amid these dynamics because it never appears urgent, as counterintuitive as that sounds.

On this point, Paul's farewell speech to the Ephesian elders in Acts 20 holds the challenge we still need today: *'Keep watch over yourselves and all the flock of which the Holy Spirit has made you overseers. Be shepherds of the church of God, which he bought with his own blood'* (Acts 20:28). These simple but profound instructions certainly sound like all-day everyday challenges to me. Keeping watch over my own life, including my discipleship, is a vital starting point for leadership; otherwise, I lose the power of leading by example and might be hypocritically pointing others boldly towards a challenge I am not trying to live myself (see *Vital sign 3* for more on this).

As Paul turns to the care of the people in the church, he uses the common biblical analogy of shepherding. Shepherds care for their sheep through their everyday 'challenges' (like not falling off cliffs or getting their heads stuck in fences), as well as their extreme ones (like being eaten by the 'savage wolves' he describes in verse 29).

Over time, the word 'overseer' here has led to a number of church titles, including presbyter, superintendent and even bishop. But before we assign this title with a status that applies to only a few senior leaders, let's keep it simple. At its heart, 'to oversee' simply means 'to keep an eye out' – not in any overly controlling way, but in the sense of care and wanting the best for each person. And that applies to anyone with a leadership role at church – senior or not, paid or not.

So, what might it look like to prioritise whole-life disciplemaking in these kinds of meetings? When I was heading up a local church, we found it helpful in our leaders' meetings to challenge each other to share our own recent frontline stories: ways we'd seen God working through us out in the world since we last met. Knowing this was going to come up in our meetings dramatically improved my prayers for interesting stories from my daily life! And I found that God graciously answered those prayers. Like the time I prayed for my neighbours and for frontline opportunities with them ('Before the next leaders' meeting – please, Lord!') and a new neighbour I had not properly spoken to leaned over the garden fence and asked if he and his wife could come and talk to me about God! Call it coincidence if you like, but it didn't happen when I wasn't praying for frontline opportunities.

After a few months of doing this 'personal story' challenge, it lost its freshness and we tried other things. Part of the answer for us was to keep finding new ways to bring whole-life discipleship back on the agenda. One of the easiest ways we found to do that was to simply put it on the agenda. Admittedly this idea isn't rocket science, but if your leaders' meetings have a list of items to discuss, the words that make it onto that page or email become vital. For a season, why not try adding 'Whole-life discipleship – challenges and opportunities for ourselves and our people' as a repeated agenda item, and see where God leads your prayerful discussions? A simple act like that can be transformational, ensuring people's mission beyond the church building receives prayerful attention alongside other strategic discussions.

One vicar of a culturally rich and diverse Anglican church in west London tried just this. He'd worked hard to embed a whole-life culture in every aspect of the church's life, so he sought to include the PCC (Parochial Church Council) too. These monthly meetings were normally taken up with the business of the church – finance, building maintenance and numbers – which is all good and necessary, but they introduced an opening fifteen-minute interaction between the leaders to talk about what God had been doing in their lives recently, on their frontlines. They would share stories and use the framework of the 6Ms of fruitfulness (see page 8) to help people think it through. Similarly, one large church in Devon with several hundred members gives agenda time in each leaders' meeting to go through a number of people in the church, pausing to pray for each one's unique frontline opportunities and challenges. The key fact remains that if leadership teams are supposed to prayerfully consider the important things in the church's life, then whole-life discipleship needs a place in the discussion.

Let me offer one slight caution, however, about making whole-life discipleship into an agenda item. Doing this can make it appear like a bolt-on to a meeting, leaving all the other items unaffected, when the whole point of whole-life discipleship is that it should not be a bolt-on but rather an integral part of everything else we do: it should colour every discussion about pastoral care, finance, appointments and so on. Nevertheless, if this slight tension is acknowledged, there's real value in intentionally scheduling it into discussions. In fact, part of the conversation it prompts can involve looking back on the other items on the agenda and asking each other if whole-life implications were sufficiently considered in each discussion.

For a well-established leadership team, all this means we're probably talking about a change in what normally happens – a culture change. As with all change, it may take time. And given the interesting human dynamics of all church leadership teams, it may be either celebrated or contested. So as with any change, it would probably be helpful for those of us with influence over what gets discussed to paint a picture of what could be. We could say something like: 'Imagine if a key part of our time together included deliberately praying for and discussing our discipleship and our people's lives beyond the gathered-church programme. What might happen if we keep looking out to the places where God has placed us, as well as looking up to him and in to the key needs of our gathered community? Imagine if we prayed for different people each time, not because they're facing a particular time of need, but because their everyday discipleship is of high value to us and to God. Imagine if we messaged them to tell them we'd taken time to pray for their frontline. Imagine if we prompted each other to share our own frontline stories and asked for updates next time we met. Could it be that this would help reframe all we do for the better?'

Pray about it

Lord, when we meet as church leaders, give us your agenda for our time together. When the temptation to look only inwards at gathered-church issues is greatest, help us to first look *up* to you and also to look *out* to your world and our people's whole lives. Whatever we're discussing, from money to maintenance, overseas mission to church-based ministries, help us to always be a disciplemaking movement. Amen.

Vital sign 12
Programme planning

In a nutshell

Whole-life discipleship doesn't happen by accident. It has to be in the plan. When planning our church programme, we need to ensure enough time and space is given to equipping people to be effective disciples in their everyday lives.

While this chapter primarily looks at planning the main teaching or preaching programme for the church, the lessons can be applied to a much wider range of things we plan. Other elements of the gathered-worship service beyond the sermon can also benefit greatly from advanced planning so that whole-life discipleship can be consciously included within them (we explored these elements in depth in *Vital sign 6*).

At the same time, when we're considering what to put on the church calendar, it's equally important to decide what *not* to add in or, indeed, what to remove. There is always the danger that we put so much into the church diary that we inadvertently prevent our people – particularly the keen ones – from spending much time on their frontlines. If a key part of the whole-life discipleship message is that we are often most strategically placed as disciples 'out there' in the world, we need to make sure we don't counteract that message by calling people back 'in here' to an ever-increasing number of gathered-church activities.

At the outset of this chapter, for any church leaders who don't feel particularly keen to plan programmes and feel, instead, that spontaneity and last-minute discernment is more their strong suit, let me offer this sporting analogy from the writer Malcolm Gladwell:

Basketball is an intricate, high-speed game filled with split-second, spontaneous decisions. But that spontaneity is possible only when everyone first engages in hours of highly repetitive and structured practice – perfecting their shooting, dribbling, and passing and running plays over and over again – and agrees to play a carefully defined role on the court . . . spontaneity isn't random.[1]

There is encouragement in this quote for me, because it rejects the idea that we have to decide between spontaneity and planning. Creativity and spontaneity can be helped rather than hindered through good plans and practices. In sport, we often see the brilliance 'in the moment', but behind that moment are plans and countless hours of preparation and practice. Likewise, if making whole-life disciples is a key goal, and one in which we fervently believe and for which we are prepared to vigorously act, we should specifically include it in our plans.

Psalm 20:4 also makes the link between the desire of our hearts and our plans: *'May he give you the desire of your heart and make all your plans succeed.'* Admittedly we would be stretching the context of this verse to say that it's referring to programme planning in church. In Psalm 20, David is under threat of attack and deeply distressed. In fact, for David, this represents a workplace setting, with battlefield and political implications, and so is very much about his whole-life discipleship. For us, planning a teaching programme is clearly a different experience – hopefully, at least. But the lesson here is nevertheless transferable, and it's one we can so easily miss. The assumption in this psalm is that we will have plans that match our desires. In this context, it's fair to ask again: if growing whole-life disciples is a desire our church professes, is it in our plans too?

In my own time as a church leader, I found it's all too easy to slip up here. In the real world, our plans are made with limited time and with the cultural backdrop of inherited church norms, traditions and expectations. Somehow, our stated priorities don't always noticeably feature in the discussion of next term's programme. When we plan our teaching series, it's not uncommon to come with a list of our own preferences, hobby horses, particular concerns, latest resources, favourite parts of the Bible, and hot topics to be discussed or avoided. As a result, other concerns take centre stage in our planning considerations, instead of intentional ways of making progress with whole-life disciplemaking.

But even when we do come with a little too much personal bias, we can be grateful that God blesses our stumbling best efforts. He can take our attempts and bless them beyond our imagination. And that means imperfect planning is better than no planning. So often a teaching plan developed months ago proves to be wonderfully timely on the day the sermon is delivered, in ways we could never have foreseen. Often, when the time comes, we find whole-life applications we haven't foreseen, and God uses our best efforts. I am always grateful that God doesn't wait for us to get everything right before he blesses our plans. Nevertheless, we should surely have plans that give our priorities the best chance of being fruitful.

In whatever way programme planning is done in your church – centralised in one person, delegated to a team, changed up every term – we're all trying to do the same thing. We're seeking God's guidance for our teaching material and Bible passages in order to bring glory to God and to help people on the journey of committing to and becoming more like Jesus. As soon as we articulate it like this, including whole-life discipleship becomes an obviously vital part of good programme planning. The 'becoming more like Jesus' element must always include people's frontline contexts. Of course, I'm not suggesting frontline mission should be the only priority, or even that all teaching planning should explicitly mention it. A church will have a number of priorities. The key question is whether enough time and space are given in the series we plan to equipping people to be effective disciples in their daily lives.

So, what might this emphasis on whole-life discipleship in sermon planning actually look like? Let's take two very different examples from neighbouring churches. Both churches believe that 'All Scripture is God-breathed and is useful for teaching, rebuking, correcting and training in righteousness' (2 Timothy 3:16), but this doesn't mean all Scripture should be given equal time in the programme. That means they have some selections to make and some planning to do. And they go about it in two very different ways.

First up, St Mark's is a rural church in Somerset. It follows the lectionary for its main Sunday service each week, which could potentially mean all this discussion about whole-life discipleship in sermon planning is redundant, at least for the main congregation. Every Sunday has allocated passages from the Old Testament, Psalms, New Testament and Proverbs. Many Church of England, Methodist, Catholic, URC and other churches follow this pattern or a similar one. So where is the potential for ensuring enough time and space is given to equipping people to be effective disciples in their everyday lives? St Mark's is committed to that vision, as well as to the wide variety of passages the lectionary brings up, and to the sense of church unity that comes from joining with others around the world in the shared lectionary.

The crux of their answer is this: being allocated a set of passages is not the same as being allocated a sermon plan or programme. There is room to discuss many themes and priorities in a way that encourages whole-life discipleship. And so, every term, the vicar of St Mark's meets with others on the preaching team and looks at the scheduled readings for the coming months. One of their key questions is whether there is a particular aspect of any of the readings that will help encourage and equip their people for the everyday contexts. The vicar is also in a WhatsApp group with a few friends and colleagues in other parishes, who are asking the same questions about the same readings. They will bring in contributions from the congregation too, to draw out insights from their everyday lives. Together, they look to share whole-life insights and stories that fit with each week's passages. This doesn't mean that every single sermon mentions frontlines, or that every Sunday has to end with a specific whole-life discipleship application. But it does mean that the team there are prayerfully looking for those opportunities and framing their sermon planning with the goal of sending people out inspired for what's to come that week.

Second, Hope Community Church is in the same village as St Mark's and is equally committed to embedding whole-life discipleship in its culture. The pastor and two other leaders meet every term to plan the teaching programme for the months ahead. Sometimes they choose to follow a book of the Bible, one section at a time, for a whole term or more. In other seasons, they'll pick themes for their preaching and suggest passages that fit those themes for each week. In some ways, Hope Community Church has more freedom to create a programme that will facilitate whole-life disciplemaking, but they have to work harder to make sure a variety of passages across the whole Bible is covered.

The pastor and leaders at Hope Community Church have a list of passages and subjects covered in recent terms and will look to ensure variety, but they will also repeat a subject or passage if they feel it is appropriate. In fact, they have a list of subjects that should be covered regularly, including specifically addressing whole-life discipleship rather than simply including it in another passage or subject. They don't feel that every term, or even every year, there has to be a specific series of 'whole-life discipleship' messages, but they do feel that every time they meet they should be asking how their sermon plan helps to equip their people as whole-life disciples. That emphasis should always be there, whether in the background or the foreground.

In your own church, then, one simple thing you could consider incorporating is a whole-life check before you confirm the sermon plan for the next season. It is sometimes useful to ask one or two trusted members of the congregation, or perhaps small-group leaders, to feed back the effectiveness of the previous programme in equipping for everyday discipleship. Their comments should also help discern whether you are on the right track. Crucially, when the new plan is taking shape, before you press 'save' or send it to the rest of the team, ask yourself: 'How likely is it this plan will help make and grow whole-life disciples?' If the response is 'very likely', great. If the honest answer is 'not very likely', then this question has done its job. The challenge is then to ask what changes could be made to bring the implications for people's daily lives back into the teaching.

Ultimately, however you plan your sermon programme, it can be a make-or-break moment for whole-life discipleship. A focus on planning provides a great opportunity to embed whole-life discipleship in the church's teaching and values.

Pray about it

Lord, as we meet to plan, help us to pause with you before we fill the spreadsheet or calendar. Help us to prayerfully picture the discipleship opportunities and challenges of our people on their frontlines. May their daily reality, and your will for each of them there, help shape the programme.

Lord, as we do our stumbling best to get this right, whatever we put down on paper or on this document, please breathe life into it. May our programmes always serve your purposes. Amen.

Vital sign 13
AGMs and annual reviews

In a nutshell

When we're tasked with reviewing the past year in our church's life, we naturally name the highlights: the things that we deem most valuable, important and noteworthy. So, does whole-life disciplemaking make the cut? If not, it probably wasn't truly a priority. But there are easy fixes for this issue, and if we deliberately include the whole-life perspective in our AGMs or annual reviews, it can be deeply significant.

Where and when do you pause to review the previous twelve months? If you don't take time as a church leader to look over your church's year, I'd politely suggest that you should. So much of our time is taken up with present needs and future plans that this can mean there is little time for past lessons. But when we do carve out time to look back, it provides the best platform for looking forward. There is a danger of dwelling in the past, whether it's glories we're holding on to or disasters, but if we don't look back at all, we miss out on too much, including the chance to assess progress towards our church's vision, hopes, dreams and God-given mission.

AGMs and annual reviews can often seem like a must-do task rather than a God-given opportunity – or is that just me? But, at their best, they provide a chance for thankfulness, as well as identifying lessons for the future so we can take forward what's been helpful and hopeful while questioning, changing or stopping anything that's not worked well. And finally, they're a brilliant, life-giving moment for thankfulness to God. Most of the time, the majority of church leaders have enough concerns and prayer needs for today and tomorrow. It's easy to forget the answers to prayers we prayed yesterday, as well as major concerns that have somehow vanished during the past year. Giving thanks to God for his provision powerfully grows our faith for the most pressing current issues. When Paul reviews his time with the church in Philippi, for example, we see his thankfulness and joy in their partnership and confidence:

I thank my God every time I remember you. In all my prayers for all of you, I always pray with joy because of your partnership in the gospel from the first day until now, being confident of this, that he who began a good work in you will carry it on to completion until the day of Christ Jesus. (Philippians 1:3–6)

Wherever they represent Jesus, our people are part of our church. And so, in the same way as Paul, when we review our church life we are surely reviewing the lives and mission of *people* in our church – and seeking reasons for thankfulness and joy wherever this good news occurs. Our confidence for the future stems from reviewing and acknowledging God at work in our past, and we can only truly know that when we take the time to look back. As Søren Kierkegaard put it: 'Life can only be understood backwards, but it must be lived forwards.'[1]

If it feels as though I'm labouring the point, please bear with me; it's worth underlining, because we're immersed in a culture that's obsessed with progress. Too often, looking back can be de-prioritised by planning ahead; the urge to do can be much stronger than the urge to review. It's a temptation we'd do well to avoid.

Thankfully, for many of us, looking back on the year is already a part of our church pattern in a variety of ways. If your church is a charity, then an AGM (or an APCM in the Church of England) and an annual report are legal requirements, and reviewing the year often happens in particular meetings – a church leaders' meeting or with the whole church. In my own Baptist church context, this included an early December review at a leaders' meeting and an AGM report in January. Sometimes, reviewing the year happens online or on paper, as a requirement of your church denomination, the charity commission or some other legislative requirement.

Equally, reviewing the year can take place personally, in our own way and our own time. When I was leading a church, that time was usually at some point between Christmas and New Year. I would make space to be alone in that week and look back on the church's year, seeking God's insights and lessons and at the same time prayerfully committing to my role for the year ahead. And a vital part of that internal, prayerful review was considering my own everyday discipleship as well as the everyday discipleship of the people in my church.

Whatever form your AGM or annual review takes, it's essential to give equal billing to the legislative requirements of running an organisation and the mission imperative of whole-life disciplemaking. Although in theory every annual review names the things that matter most, in practice we often end up naming whatever is most noticeable. That means we default to listing calendar events, church programme items and church community initiatives. All these are good and should be highlighted, but when we explain our purpose, does it explicitly include making and encouraging disciples to live out their faith in all of life? Do we give account for the ways in which we've helped to deliver on this vision, and assess the extent to which we've achieved it this year? If not, here are two simple shifts that can contribute significantly towards correcting the situation:

1 Review goals, not just things

We need to make sure we look back not just at what we've done, but at what we were trying to achieve. I always found it much easier to review the list of activities, events and programmes, but if we frame that list with what we're trying to achieve, we'll be able to contextualise these things, determining whether they actually did the work of equipping God's people for daily mission, or we've slipped back into a 'gathered-church-only' mindset.

2 Measure what you can

Don't be put off by the fact that whole-life discipleship isn't easily measurable in the way church events and attendance are. Much of the 'soft' outcome of our work is hard to measure, but this should never be an excuse for emphasising the more easily measured aspects instead. We can ask our people the extent to which they feel equipped and encouraged for their frontlines, for example: a story of God working through someone in their job will fit just as well within a review of the year as the number of people who came to an outdoor carol service or the number we helped in our foodbank. It's a great idea, therefore, to collect stories throughout the year that can be included whenever we come to an annual review. On top of that, we can report on the things that have made space for whole-life discipleship to thrive – the chapters of this book should give you some ideas for what those could be.

Of course, you might be thinking, 'Who pays attention to these reviews, anyway?' AGMs and annual reviews are often seen more as a logistics hoop to jump through than a welcome moment of thankfulness and purpose. But the reality is that some *will* listen to what you say on the stage or write in the report. Far from mindless admin work, annual reviews are a line in the sand; manifestos that either reinvigorate people for their part in the mission of the church or reinforce a 'building-centric' approach. Imagine how encouraging it will be if we choose to draw attention to the way our church is sending people out each week to join God's work in the world; the way our community has spent the year taking part in the restoration of all things, in hundreds of different places, relationships and tasks. Those attending will expect us to say much about events we've held and ministries we've run, and we will. But we can also send a significant and encouraging message if our report on the year deliberately includes whole-life examples – underlining that what happens Monday to Saturday is every bit as important, wonderful and worth celebrating as what happens on Sunday.

Here's how that looks in one church in South Yorkshire. They have about 100 members, and usually welcome about 150 adults to Sunday services. The minister and leaders have used LICC resources for a few years and are increasingly committed to embedding whole-life discipleship in the culture of their church. Until recently, this hadn't translated into the various ways they review their year, so the leaders resolved to make some changes. In the past few years, this church has introduced several initiatives to make sure whole-life discipleship is front and centre when the AGM rolls around.

First, one of the leaders has been charged with the role of 'whole-life champion'. Throughout the year, if others forget to consider a particular activity's implications for life beyond the gathered church, it's their role to bring those implications back to the top of the agenda. As a result, when it comes to reviewing the year, it's much more natural to include whole-life disciplemaking in the picture, because every meeting over the previous twelve months has included discussion of how the church is equipping people for everyday mission.

Second, when they're planning content for the AGM, they always look for a frontline example to sit alongside each gathered-church example. When they talk about their church's value of justice, for instance, they include stories from their partnership with charities like Tearfund *and* from members of the congregation who have stood up for justice in their daily lives, like the manager who's tackled the culture of unpaid overtime in her workplace. When they consider their Christ-like-caring value, they'll include a report on their foodbank *and* the story of the family who've quietly been doing the housework for their struggling neighbour all year. When they consider their value of sharing the message of hope, they review their Alpha courses and special guest services *and* share stories of the parents who are growing relationships during the school drop-off and speaking to others about their faith. They'll note a baptism that didn't take place in their church at all but in a nearby town, because of their people's positive influence on that person. It's not hard to imagine the impact this has on their culture;

the message is heard loud and clear that the gathered and scattered lives of the church are both equally important to the leadership – and to God.

Finally, the desire to share these kinds of specific whole-life examples also means they've had to implement a culture of *looking* for these stories throughout the year. What are the key challenges, opportunities and encouragements their people are facing each week? How is the body of the church getting on outside the building, and what is God doing through his people in local streets, workplaces, pubs, clubs, gyms and homes? They have these conversations as a matter of deliberate policy throughout the year, and then, as part of their desire that all their people would be equipped to be salt and light in their everyday contexts, at AGM time they share what comes up. Wherever examples of fruitfulness occur they are celebrated; and if the leaders are struggling to find examples to share, then they treat that as a legitimate concern in itself. Is there a lack of stories, or are the leaders not listening closely enough to hear them?

I know I didn't always grasp these opportunities, but there's a winning combination here that would have helped – finding another key leader to champion the cause, looking to include whole-life examples alongside the more noticeable scattered ones and collecting whole-life stories throughout the year. Making any one of these changes would be significant.

Pray about it

Lord, I recognise the danger of reviewing what's most noticeable at the expense of what's most important. Help us to review our church's disciplemaking with your eyes. Remind us of this year's whole-life challenges and this year's whole-life stories.

As we review, help us to honestly assess progress, learn your lessons for the future, and give you thanks and praise for the hundreds of frontline victories our people have seen this year. And as we note progress made on our frontlines, helps us to be confident that you who began a good work will carry it on to completion until the day of Christ Jesus. Amen.

Vital sign 14
Communications

In a nutshell

We communicate what we don't want people to miss. If we're committed to growing whole-life disciples, it will be unmissable across our range of communications, from news sheets to social media and beyond.

Church communications take many forms, from news sheets and verbal notices, through emails, texts and social media, all the way to bespoke church apps. Churches vary in how they do things, but all churches have communications. In fact, not just churches; we all communicate, whether that's verbally, through body language or in writing. We're always communicating something. And others are receiving those messages, picking up those signals – whether consciously or unconsciously. Often, what we don't say can communicate as much as what we do.

It is therefore a vital sign of a whole-life disciplemaking church when our commitment to that vision is included in our regular communications. But we'll probably need to work hard to include items related to whole-life discipleship in them. In fact, even if you've picked up this book full of energy for whole-life disciplemaking, I still might have to work hard to convince you that it should (or can) be inescapable in your news sheets, social posts and emails. Aren't our communication channels just for announcing what's going on? Do we *really* need to bang the whole-life discipleship drum there too?

Let's explore that question briefly. There are two main types of church communications, and two main arguments for why whole-life discipleship doesn't quite fit within them. First, there are communications about the upcoming programme of events in church life, aimed at those who are already part of the church. Some may argue that these notices are essentially about our various gathered-church activities rather than the scattered life of the church – that this is a place where it's OK to be sacred–secular divided. After all, what are we going to announce – every congregation member's personal calendar?

Second, there are communications pitched at those outside the church community, or on the fringes of it, often delivered through social media or the church's website. Here, it could be argued that including messages 'from the church' about our roles as missionaries in daily life might be confusing for those who haven't yet joined in with any of the church's gathered activities.

While these points have some validity, let me make a couple of counterpoints. First, when it comes to gathered-church communications, this isn't an either/or issue. Of course, the majority of our comms will cover gathered-church events and activities, but if they only ever include this sort of information, we may be unintentionally devaluing people's roles outside of the church's gathered activities. People notice what does and doesn't get spotlighted, even if subconsciously. If we're trying to build a church culture that inspires people to see God at work in their daily lives, then that change must extend to the words and messages we transmit. In short, we shouldn't let what we choose to communicate work against everything else we do, reinforcing the idea that gathered church takes priority over our scattered lives.

Second, when it comes to our outward-facing communications, the whole-life message actually has a positive impact rather than a puzzling one. Far from being something non-Christians won't understand, messaging about whole-life discipleship, if framed correctly, may be the very thing that draws people in. It could be the missing ingredient they're looking for: a faith that has something to say to and makes sense of the whole of their lives. Generally, those who find faith for the first time don't need an induction into the idea that discipleship covers all of their lives.

In truth, it's usually those coming from other churches who have inherited a strong and thriving sacred–secular divide who might need more help to understand your church's whole-life emphasis. The greater danger for communication with non-Christians is the message conveyed by a gathered-centric approach – that joining this community essentially means attending a lot of stuff, rather than following Jesus through life.

If we don't make a conscious effort to craft our communications with whole-life vision in their DNA, there's a very real danger that we will drift back to implying an unhelpful hierarchy of 'important' or 'spiritual' jobs. If the only roles mentioned in our communications involve serving in church, then we may be saying more than we mean to. I know the pressure of constantly trying to fill multiple vacancies in the much-needed areas of service in church life. These must, of course, be given a profile. But I also know we need to keep a healthy balance by including communications about the many roles people hold as disciples out in the world: carers, employees, friends, team captains, chairs, organisers, drivers, builders and so on.

In essence, our communications offer the chance to redress the balance on what we count as good news stories and who we consider spiritual heroes. If we expand their remit just a little, we can use them to celebrate and tell stories from those in all walks of life – from students and parents to workers and retirees. Although a message about someone's frontline, a whole-life inspiring quote or a workplace prayer may not currently be obvious candidates for our communications, they can be very powerful.

This approach has biblical foundations. In Ephesians 4:29, Paul writes, *'Do not let any unwholesome talk come out of your mouths, but only what is helpful for building others up according to their needs, that it may benefit those who listen.'* He's clearly not talking about social media or the church news sheet here; he's talking about talking. Nevertheless, the challenge can be applied more widely. When it comes to our church communications let's find words that are helpful for building others up, and benefit them according to their needs. Those needs absolutely include the pressures and opportunities they face as Christians out in God's world. And let's be mindful that 'unwholesome talk' includes discouraging words. If what we communicate reinforces the idea that someone's time at work or with friends is of secondary importance to their time at church, that's unlikely to be encouraging.

The best answer here is not the easiest. The easiest thing is to throw a 'whole-life slot' somewhere into the regular church communications. That's far better than not including it at all, but it has its problems. A discrete slot runs counter to the idea that the whole-life discipleship vision is in the DNA of the church. There is a better way. Not just a one-off nod that follows the same format every time, but a commitment to weaving the theme into different communication across different weeks. Let's explore some concrete examples of what that might look like.

Prayer requests

Most churches have a way to communicate prayer requests and/or news of answered prayers, whether from the front of church, in a prayer sheet or WhatsApp group, in small groups and so on. Once in a while, it's possible to include a message like this: 'Alongside these prayers, let's remember to pray for our people's frontlines, for the everyday challenges and opportunities they face. Ask the Lord to bring to your mind someone in our church to pray for in their everyday context this week.'

Even when our prayers focus on those who are struggling, there is space to acknowledge and include those struggling on their frontline. Depending on the size of your church and the nature of the issue for prayer, this could be very specific prayer for a named person, or quite general. For example: 'Let's pray for those in our church who are really struggling at work or on other frontlines at the moment, including those who desperately want to be led to a different workplace. Lord, please guide, comfort and strengthen them. While we join them in seeking a better context and fit for their gifts, please also give them strength for this week. Show them they still have a role in your master plan today.'

Thoughts for the day

If you share encouraging or thought-provoking quotes and ideas with your congregation, maybe via social media or a regular email, don't just stick to words from well-known speakers and authors. You can also include quotes from people in your church, or people known to you, about the ways they've seen God working in their everyday life. For example, in describing what they'd learned about whole-life discipleship, someone recently said to me, 'Every time we go out of the front door – and sometimes when we don't – who we are and what we do witnesses for Jesus, for better or worse.' With permission and perhaps anonymity, quotes like this are eminently quotable and they help people to see their ordinary places through God's eyes, and also underline that we all have wisdom to share – not just the leaders.

Sermon links

It's easy for our comms to be purely focused on what's coming up, but sometimes we can maximise a message by going back over what's already happened. So, if our midweek communications look back at Sunday's sermon, can we ask how people are applying the lessons in their everyday life? If these allow for wider participation, like comments and shared dialogue (a WhatsApp group, for example), then encouraging people to share examples of applying last week's sermon to our frontlines will be particularly powerful.

Community magazines

If your church distributes regular community round-ups or magazines to the homes in your area, you could plan to include whole-life discipleship messages in the mix of content. That might look like telling a story of how God has worked through someone in the church over the last month, writing a short thought about each of the 6Ms of fruitfulness in turn (see page 8 for more on those).

Website

Given that so many people find their way to our websites as a first port of call, what do they find out about our heart there? Is it obvious that we want to help them discover the value and purpose in all they do, including beyond our church gatherings? The rule of thumb we discussed at the start of this section also applies here: integrating a whole-life vision across the website is far preferable to creating a separate 'whole-life discipleship' section or page. Wherever you describe who you are, your gatherings, your vision and aims, or your activities, there's your opportunity to explain how the gathered life of the church is focused outwards, to our scattered mission.

Here are two examples to prompt your own thoughts:

You might be a plumber or a teacher, retired or a student, unemployed or seeking different employment. Your interests might include sport or films, the arts or science, the great outdoors or the armchair. We believe all these contexts and places matter to God, and we seek to encourage and equip you to follow Jesus well through all the opportunities and challenges you have there.

This is the list of our church's activities, but it's not a list of all we do as a church. Every day, in hundreds of contexts, our people are out and about, modelling godly character, making good work, ministering grace and love, moulding culture, and being mouthpieces for truth and justice and messengers of the gospel. Day by day, we seek to support, encourage and pray for them.

Many of our online communications will be seen and read by our people while they are on their frontlines. If we were to prayerfully picture this when composing our messages, how might they change?

Social media

As well as applying the ideas above to our social media presence, it's also worth considering our personal channels. For some church leaders, personal social feeds are kept entirely separate from their church friends, while for others they're deeply integrated. To the extent that our church family view what we post and comment on, are we encouraging a whole-life perspective on discipleship? LICC posts regularly on multiple social media platforms; it could just be that resharing one of our posts is exactly the encouragement someone in your church needs, and it might carry more weight because you've drawn attention to it.

You can probably think of other communications categories too. The list above may already seem daunting, but this can equally be an area where we score a quick win. Is there one area of your church communication where whole-life discipleship could be more intentionally included this week?

Pray about it

Lord, please give us the words and show us the ways to communicate our whole-life discipleship message and stories. May our words neither overstate the current reality nor undersell our resolve to equip people for their frontlines. Amen.

Vital Sign 15
Annual opportunities

In a nutshell

If we provide an annual opportunity to focus on whole-life discipleship, it can be an extremely powerful way to embed this thinking in our church. Equally, there's also the potential to achieve almost nothing if it stays an isolated event with no follow-up through the year. If we take these opportunities at weekends away, leaders' away days, or special services to communicate the whole-life vision, and then respond to them by backing them up afterwards, the impact can be significant.

Coming up with a title for this chapter was tricky! 'Annual opportunity' is a bit of a catch-all term, but in essence I'll use it here to refer to yearly moments in the church calendar when we make space for a more focused engagement with the idea and practice of whole-life discipleship. These moments can take a variety of forms. They could be church leaders coming together to consider whole-life discipleship on a retreat, or a focused whole-church weekend, or perhaps a special Sunday devoted to frontlines, like a commissioning service. Of course, if the frequency of these events is less or more than yearly in your case, the lessons here will still apply.

And right at the outset, here's a warning: these kinds of annual opportunities can be a great support to whole-life disciplemaking, but if they are the only time in the year when the vision is emphasised and encouraged, they will be received as tokenism. While it would be legitimate to hold a leaders' away day to launch or re-embed the church's whole-life emphasis, or to run a Sunday service with a 'from this point on' feel, the danger comes if we introduce an annual whole-life weekend or service that has no connection with the year just gone and no influence on the year ahead. For example, I once visited a church for a service in which they absolutely nailed the whole-life message, but after that they never returned to the theme in any noticeable way again.

With that caveat made, though, sometimes a specific, focused annual event looking at whole-life discipleship helps the message to break through when many might have missed the whole-life discipleship values week by week. The whole-life message is essential but subtle, vital but easily missed. An annual event is a good opportunity to check that everyone understands how vital this is; not to add one more activity into the already crowded church programme, but to give a clear sign of the significance we want to recognise in people's everyday ministry.

For some churches, annual days or weekends focusing on different causes and priorities are already part of their regular rhythm. For example, if you already have a special Sunday for certain other missions – for your foodbank or for overseas missionaries, for example – imagine the power of having a parallel Sunday that highlights the fact that *all* your people are missionaries to their daily contexts. Or equally, imagine the effect of never doing this. There's a danger we effectively express the view that the missions that really matter are the 'other ones'; that the missionaries who come with prayer letters on the board are the proper ones. It's worth considering the overall message these Sundays communicate. Likewise, if you often hold leaders' retreats or a church weekend away (or similar), consider the impact of the themes and topics you select for talks and study. Are you giving people a sense that they're gathering to be inspired to join in with what God's doing in their daily lives, or that they're escaping from the 'secular world' into a brief moment with him?

Throughout the Bible, God's people show they have terrible memories. They forget what he has done, as well as what they're supposed to do. We are no different. Thankfully, there are many Old Testament examples of how we can create patterns to help us remember the important things. Stones are placed where they'll remind Israel of key events, symbols are tied on hands or foreheads, notes are written on doorframes or gates, meals are established to remember God's provision – most notably, the Passover meal: 'This is a day you are to commemorate; for the generations to come you shall celebrate it as a festival to the LORD – a lasting ordinance' (Exodus 12:14).

My memory is no better than theirs. If they needed patterns to remember the escape from Egypt as 'a lasting ordinance', I know I need patterns to focus on the key aspects of my discipleship journey too. Annual services or retreats can play a key part in that process. Whole-life discipleship should be embedded in every part of our church's life, but we can all benefit from annual reminders of the centrality, wonder and urgency of the whole-life gospel. We all need to be shaken out of our stupor every once in a while!

As an example, one church in the New Forest uses Plough Sunday as its annual opportunity to refocus on whole-life discipleship. Plough Sunday is the day in the Anglican liturgical calendar when a plough was traditionally brought into the sanctuary and the community dedicated their ploughing to God, seeking his help and his blessing for the work that was so vital to their very existence. As it happens, this church is neither Anglican nor in a particularly agricultural area, but they do recognise the value and power of the symbolism involved.

They bring a plough to the front of the building, but alongside it there will also be computer keyboards and corporate coffee mugs, Nordic walking poles, football boots, ladders and a mop, van keys and Allen keys, schoolbooks and stethoscopes ... all brought by the people who use them in their week. Each person will dedicate the work of their hands, home and away, paid and unpaid, to the Lord their God, in the hearing of their fellow believers. And each person will be commissioned for their work, in the presence of their church family.

This communal act links to the church's whole-life values throughout the year, powerfully reminds people of their frontline discipleship, and sends them out encouraged for the day, week, month and year ahead. As they face the year ahead, Plough Sunday reminds them all of their total dependence on God, and that whatever they do, they are doing it with and for him.

This is a simple but powerful way to run an annual opportunity that really changes people's perspective on their daily life and mission. It's also an easy one to adopt in your own church. When it comes to the commissioning words, you can use whatever fits your church's style and culture; but to help you reflect on the way a service like this could work for you, let's look at some components and wording for a commissioning service that could be adapted for your particular context.

Commissioning words

[*Leader*] Will you pray that God's presence will be experienced on your frontline?
[*All*] **By the grace of God we will.**

Will you search for his will and let it be done in your day-to-day decisions and deeds?
By the grace of God we will.

Will you reflect what it means to be a follower of Jesus in all your relationships?
By the grace of God we will.

Will you live in such a way that others will be pointed to the gospel of the Lord Jesus Christ?
By the grace of God we will.

Will you make a conscious effort to minister and witness across all types of barriers in a sympathetic, loving and patient manner?
By the grace of God we will.

When conditions allow, will you invite others to acknowledge Christ as Lord?
By the grace of God we will.

On behalf of all of us, I commend you to this work and pledge to you our prayers, encouragement and support. May the Holy Spirit guide and strengthen you, that in this and in all things you may do God's will to the service of Jesus Christ. And may he be with you, this day and all the days of your life. Amen.

Father, thank you for the offer of new life in Christ. Thank you for giving my life renewed purpose – for transforming the way I see my daily work, my relationships and my leisure time. Thank you for all those who have showed and shared your good news with me. Now, Lord, help me to live a fruitful life in and through my work on the frontline that you have called me to. Lord, through me would you draw others to know you; stretch out your mighty hand to do great works in the places where I work, and give me the courage and the presence of mind to share you each day through my actions, speech and behaviour. For your glory may it be so. Amen.

The resources that go with this book are designed to provide help for an annual opportunity for church leaders. In particular, the *Vital Signs Assessment Tool* (see page 11 for more information) can be helpful as part of an annual church leaders' retreat or day.

Each leader can give their own answers to the twenty questions beforehand, or at the start of the day together, and then the overall scores and implications can be shared among the group as part of a day thinking and praying together.

Whether it is time spent with church leaders, a special annual service or a church weekend, this focused annual opportunity can achieve so much to help embed whole-life discipleship in our churches. It can renew our vision and resolve, offer opportunities to review and set targets, and provide a reminder and a chance to prayerfully commit each other's frontlines to God for the year ahead.

Pray about it

Lord, I recognise my own ability to forget the important things. Show me the annual opportunities that would be most effective for helping us commit or recommit to whole-life discipleship in our church this year. Help me to carve out the time to consider whole-life discipleship with my leaders, and celebrate whole-life discipleship with all our people. Amen.

Section 4

WHEN WE RESPOND

Vital sign 16
When the frontline comes to us

In a nutshell

As church leaders, sometimes our frontline is found on the doorstep, among those who regularly walk through our church doors. And sometimes, especially if our church doesn't have its own building, our frontline ministry is in the times when we walk through their doors. It's easy to be so busy on these occasions that we forget to ask our God: 'How could I be more fruitful on those frontlines?'

There's the Slimming World group that hires our hall every week. There's Mary, who delivers the post to church every day. There's Abdul the photocopier engineer, whom we see surprisingly often, and Bill, who checks the fire extinguishers and alarm systems each year. There's Steph the cleaner, who might spend more hours on her knees in church than anyone else. There's Sam the pub landlady, who hires out her function room every Thursday for our young adult event. Add up all these incidental contacts, and the list of people we engage with through church business is surprisingly large.

In my own life, the person who totally changed my perspective on these encounters was Mark, who was, funnily enough, a photocopier engineer. The photocopier was in my office, and it was being problematic (read 'evil'). I was, frankly, busy. I showed Mark in and offered him a drink. He was new to our church building and something told me he wasn't entirely happy to be there. I wanted – actually, I *needed* – to get on with my work. But here was this man in my office, doing battle with the photocopier. So we started chatting.

After some time and a lot of frustration, Mark got to the nub of the problem with the photocopier, but not before he'd shared his problem with church. He told me he used to go to church in a town about thirty minutes away – a great, thriving church that I happened to know.

'My brother has special needs,' he explained. 'As a kid, he couldn't sit still or be quiet. He would make noises. Someone from the church turned around and told us all off for the noise he was making. And I've never been back.'

At that moment, I didn't know the circumstances or the other side of the story. I didn't know who spoke to them and whether they were a regular part of the church. But none of that mattered. I apologised to Mark in the most unequivocal and sincere way I could, and explained the way I hoped he and his brother would be treated if they were in my church. He didn't sign the membership form there and then, but our relationship changed from that point on. And his interactions with our church – of which there were many, because we had a terrible photocopier – also changed. He seemed much more comfortable in our office after that.

The point I'm making is this: whenever we regularly interact with people who aren't Christians, that's a frontline for us. But in calling these interactions frontlines, there's a balancing act to perform, a tightrope to walk. We can fall off this tightrope on either side before we even realise it's there. Let's explore this balancing issue, so we can place our weight and emphasis in the right place.

As we've seen, frontlines are places where we regularly spend time with those who don't follow Jesus, places where we naturally show up, usually beyond the gathered church. But for those of us in full-time church roles and/or who spend most of our time with Christians, our frontlines may sometimes be different from everyone else's. Rather than a place of work or some other place where we spend *most* of our time, they're more likely to be somewhere we spend *less* of our time. They might include places where we volunteer, like being a school governor, or leisure activities we're part of, like a sports team. And sometimes they include the times described in this chapter, when our work means we connect with individuals and organisations that are not part of the church.

All of which brings us to the balancing act. Can those of us in full-time church positions describe our *own* frontlines in a way that doesn't encourage others to think of their time volunteering in church programme activities as *their* main frontline? Likewise, can we help our people understand the difference between volunteering at church-led community activities and their everyday frontlines? Church community activity is brilliant, but if that's our only example of a frontline, we perpetuate the sacred–secular divide and the idea that church-based activities are the only place mission really happens. If we're not careful, we can give the idea that our people can come and 'do their frontline' with the church and then leave and get on with the rest of their lives. If we do this, we will have lost the vital point about whole-life discipleship – that it's about the whole of our lives rather than just our voluntary time.

The reason this distinction matters is that too many people in church spend too much time in gathered-church activities. We can give the impression that time in church and with Christians is what matters most. Gathered-church activities are, of course, a key part of our mission. Wisdom is always required to discern the right ones to purpose and the right number of them to place in the calendar. But generally, at the moment, too many Christians spend too much time with Christians. Whole-life discipleship is the antidote to this, pointing out the missional value of our whole week, of all our tasks and relationships and places. The word 'frontline' points us outwards – so if we define it purely in terms of gathered-church activities, we will have fallen off one side of the tightrope.

Equally, though, if we fail to acknowledge that, for some, there are genuinely times when the frontline comes to us – like when Mark the photocopier engineer is called out to the church office – it would be to ignore some vital opportunities and fall off the other side of the tightrope.

There are two simple tests we can use to check whether we've got this balance right:

1 When we talk about the frontlines that come to us as church leaders, can we also point to at least some other personal frontlines that are fully outside of the church building and programme?

2 When we think of those who come into our spaces and the times we go into theirs, can we readily think of examples of the 6Ms of fruitfulness (page 8)?

The bottom line is summed up in Colossians 3:17: *'And whatever you do, whether in word or deed, do it all in the name of the Lord Jesus, giving thanks to God the Father through him.'* All our words and actions are to be said or done in Jesus' name. In a very real way, we represent him in all our encounters with people. I've seen hundreds of outstanding examples in churches across the UK. Acts of kindness for those who come into our building to service the boiler or hire the hall, for example, showing people they matter in every encounter.

Simple things speak volumes. They speak about us, but they also speak about our Lord and Saviour. This might be one of the few interactions this particular maintenance firm has with a church, so our words and actions may constitute a large part of what they have to go on when they consider who Jesus is and how his followers behave. That means our timing in paying bills, our understanding of the other person's work pressures, and the state in which we leave spaces we hire all count.

To see how this looks in a bit more detail, let's consider Balham Baptist Church, a city-based community that takes regular rental bookings for its space, seeing almost 2,000 different people walk through the doors each week. They have decided to adopt an intentional posture towards the groups that use their building on a weekly basis and the professionals who visit it, coming to see that their facility is a key frontline for them. Their church manager, Leisa, co-ordinates the small team that serves on this frontline – a frontline that comes to them as they find themselves meeting Lou and Jakub the binmen, or Dave who comes to service the fire alarm, or Kalisa the postwoman, or Jermaine the Amazon delivery driver, or Seonaid who runs singing lessons, or Nick the pest-control specialist (she definitely needs to keep him sweet). As she and her team interact with all these people, the 6Ms of fruitfulness (page 8) have really helped shape their approach.

1 Modelling godly character

Managing twenty-four groups and the comings and goings of so many people requires levels of patience and self-control that a monk would be proud of. But as Leisa liaises over access to keys, and smooths the transitions between groups using rooms, she shows gentleness to those who get frustrated, as well as kindness to the postwoman who wants to drop the letters but also use 'the facilities' on her round.

2 Making good work

A key element of Leisa's work is setting up lease agreements and short-term contracts to give the best user experience. This requires her to be nimble, clear, prompt and fair in all her communications with the various businesses and charities she deals with. Negotiating a cheaper rate for the first six months has enabled a number of smaller businesses to get off the ground, and working to create clear long-term agreements has meant established businesses like the nursery can be more certain about their future.

3 Ministering grace and love

Leisa knows most of the hirers and service-people by name and takes time to talk with them. When they come into the church building, she's the ambassador they meet. She's got to know about the birth of their children, the loss of a parent, the pressures of their work – she aims to be good news to them, and when appropriate she tells them she'll be praying for them. She wants them to know that God is good and the church isn't bad!

As just one example of the difference this approach has made, Jermaine from Amazon shared with Leisa that his mother had passed away and he was having to travel to be at her funeral in Jamaica. Leisa felt a prompt to help, so with one or two other neighbours, she put together a financial gift to help him with the costs he incurred at this difficult time.

4 Moulding culture

In order to create a welcoming and safe space, Leisa's team invested in a decent coffee machine and turned the sanctuary into a hub where people could meet or wait for their group to start. Hirers describe the facility as warm and friendly, and they look forward to running their groups there. In fact, their own approach to their work is influenced by the culture the church has created.

5 Being a Mouthpiece for truth and justice

Taking bookings might seem simple, but Leisa and the team know otherwise. Problems occur, mistakes are made, and misunderstandings happen on both sides. Being a mouthpiece for truth and justice means disagreements are handled as fairly and appropriately as possible. Sometimes a booking arrangement has to be stopped. Viewing these interactions as a frontline, and representing Jesus, does not mean anything goes or should be consistently tolerated. When an arrangement has to end, Leisa seeks to do it with truth and justice, and with as much kindness as possible, even if it isn't received that way!

6 Being a Messenger of the gospel

Over time those who book the building have come to view Leisa and the team as safe and friendly people they can speak freely to or, on occasion, ask about the big questions of life and faith. Leisa will offer a warm invitation to join in with the other things the church does, whether that's the Christmas appeal for a charity they support or joining them at an Easter service. People never feel pressured, or that their relationship will be affected if they can't make it this time.

So often, our frontline opportunities are closer to home than we imagine. The challenge for all of us is to represent our Saviour well, whenever and wherever these opportunities arise.

Pray about it

Lord, I'm pausing to pray for the frontlines that come to us and the frontlines my church work takes me into. Help me to represent you well in those places and moments. As we open doors to others or as they open doors for us, would you open up conversations and hearts.

May these frontlines be more fruitful this year as we seek to model godly character, make good work, minister grace and love, mould culture, and be mouthpieces for truth and justice and messengers of the gospel. Amen.

Vital sign 17
Times of transition

In a nutshell

All jobs, paid and unpaid, matter to God, but not all new jobs are equally acknowledged. The way key moments of transition in people's lives are acknowledged and celebrated will often say more about the church's whole-life discipleship values than anything we say in a sermon.

When he was first appointed as Archbishop of Canterbury, Justin Welby was interviewed and asked about his work in the oil industry before he was ordained as a church minister. He said:

> Being in a world where almost no one, the vast majority of people were not Christian believers, and the challenge of working out what being a Christian meant in that world was hugely, hugely important and taught me to value that everyone has a vocation. Everyone is called to be a Christian disciple wherever they are. It is not just for people who get ordained.[1]

Of course he's right, we know he's right, but when someone in our church is called to a new 'wherever they are', how do we recognise that? How do we mark it? If the person is ordained and their new 'wherever they are' is a church ministry role, chances are there will be a whole service to celebrate it. In fact, even if someone in the church is doing a gap year or short-term mission with a Christian organisation, it's highly likely to be profiled at the front of church and prayed for – and rightly so.

So, what about the young person in your church doing a gap year or overseas summer role *not* with a Christian organisation? I'm guilty of not always giving them equal profile, but I am seeking to redress that in future. We know that their discipleship challenges aren't any easier and their need for prayer isn't any less.

And what about the rest of us, whenever we move jobs, roles or contexts, when we're made redundant or when we retire? Clearly, it wouldn't be practical to have a service of celebration and commissioning for every key moment of transition for everyone in our church. So how do we mark these occasions in ways that communicate their equal importance? And how can we make sure we pray for our people at these pivotal moments in their whole-life discipleship?

The size of our church will be a key factor in what's possible and appropriate. The main Sunday gathering won't be the right place for many churches; small groups might be more appropriate. Some churches, though, are small enough to celebrate birthdays in the Sunday service, but would never think to celebrate a new job or other frontline role change.

Picture a person attending their church on Sunday and looking ahead to starting a new job on Monday. You know what's on their mind. They almost certainly come wanting, hoping and praying for some message of relevance and encouragement for their new start somewhere during the service, but would it even occur to them to mention what's going on to the leaders? If the answer is 'yes', that's an encouraging, healthy start. If the answer is 'probably not' or 'certainly not everyone would', what could we do to change the norms and make it clear that we'd love to hear this sort of news? How do we make sure everyone knows that we want to pray for them at times like this – not necessarily in a public way if that would make them feel uncomfortable, but to support them?

Perhaps a good start would be considering the special services or slots for paid church roles. When we run those, can we include a mention or even a prayer of commissioning for everyone else – for their roles outside of the gathered church? Some churches have much more flexibility than others here, but to the extent that you are able to do this, it can be very powerful.

Some years ago, LICC gave away badges in seminars with the initials 'FTCW' ('Full Time Christian Worker'). They were designed to prompt conversation and reinforce the message that this title applies to all of us; the only qualifying criterion is to commit our whole lives, our 'wherever' contexts, to God. One church subsequently bought a few hundred of these badges for the commissioning of a new youth pastor in the church. During this pastor's commissioning, they gave everyone present a badge explaining the meaning and message. Alongside the prayers for the new youth role, there was a prayer of commissioning for everyone attending, sending them out to their own frontlines. While the element of surprise only worked once and the badges were used in just that one service, this pattern of commissioning everyone is now used whenever someone is employed by the church and celebrated at a special induction service.

Whenever we do come to know about a new role or time of transition, we can use this example as a prompt to ask to be informed about others. Imagine an announcement along these lines: 'Abeni starts a new job tomorrow, her first since graduating. We're going to pray for her. As a church, we believe that new roles and changes in roles like this are vital times in our discipleship, and we'd love to know whenever that's the case for you. Rest assured, if you tell us, we won't embarrass you with a prayer from the front unless you're OK with that! But I hope you know, if you come here, that we're committed to valuing all of the places God calls us to, and we love to pray for people – commissioning them into the new contexts he's given them.'

Or, if we know about this opportunity in advance, there's room to do something bespoke and creative. Imagine Abeni is starting a job as an engineer. Could we phone or email a Christian engineer we know and ask them for some appropriate words – how might they pray for people in that industry? Or is there someone in your church just coming up to retirement? As well as praying for them in this key moment of transition, could we ask them what prayers they would have wanted at the start of their career that might bless Abeni?

Here is another example of how this has worked. Every year, at the beginning of September, the church in Balham that was mentioned in the last chapter would take time in their Sunday worship to mark the moment their children and young people moved up in their youth groups. Usually a gift was given, like a Bible or a Christian book. However, once the church had caught the vision for whole-life discipleship, they began to think about the truth that God was interested in the subjects their children were studying at school, and the potential careers these would lead to. They wanted to shift from an obvious sacred–secular division (celebrating Sunday school transition but not ordinary school transition), so they changed their tradition from 'Going Up Sunday' to 'Schoolbag Sunday'. In these services, they used the slogan 'We're with you' to let the children and youth know that the church community was thinking of them during the week.

They also gave them rulers and pencils with the 'We're with you' slogan on them, as a gift they could take into school without getting embarrassed (much better than 'Smile, Jesus Loves you' stickers!). This got the church thinking about commissioning in a new way, and it kickstarted a 'commissioning culture'. The leaders made a point of finding out when anyone was going through a significant life transition and then commissioning them as a church family: new job, promotion, moving house, passing a career qualification – they would tell the story in their service and then pray for them.

These are just a few ideas – the possibilities go on! For example, we can also grab the moment and pray whenever we hear of these new starts, including before the service and afterwards over coffee. Or if we normally offer prayer ministry after the service, these key changes in frontlines can be one of the things we deliberately include when we mention the availability of prayer.

As well as thinking about gathered services, we can also consider how small groups can celebrate and support people in their life transitions. For example, we can give small-group leaders words and suggestions to help make their closing prayers feel more like a commissioning event. As with all these things, the wording and style needs to fit your church culture, but here's something for starters, adapted from the Church of England's prayers for the first day of work or school:

O God, who works and gives us work, thank you for giving
[name] this new job.
We stand with them and we pray for them.
May this new start bring new blessings.
As they begin and when they continue, make known your will
for them in this role.
Help them to discover friends among strangers,
to meet opportunities and challenges eagerly,
and to do all their daily tasks in your name.
May they bring your salt and light to their role and the
workplace.
Help them to increasingly
- Model godly character;
- Make good work;
- Minister grace and love;
- Mould the culture of their workplace;
- be a Mouthpiece for truth and justice; and
- be a Messenger of the gospel.

Give them strength to overcome their worries,
and preserve them in your safekeeping,
through Jesus Christ our Lord.[2]
Amen.

When commissioning prayer like this happens in the small group,
leaders can back it up with a phone call or message, assuring the
people concerned of the church's prayers and asking how the first
week has gone.

Another approach is to focus on a passage that picks up on this
theme of commissioning. Matthew 5:13–16 is a great one to discuss
and pray through for these moments of transition:

'You are the salt of the earth. But if the salt loses its saltiness,
how can it be made salty again? It is no longer good for
anything, except to be thrown out and trampled underfoot.
You are the light of the world. A town built on a hill cannot be

hidden. Neither do people light a lamp and put it under a bowl.
Instead, they put it on its stand, and it gives light to everyone
in the house. In the same way, let your light shine before others,
that they may see your good deeds and glorify your Father in
heaven.'

Exactly what Jesus meant by the disciples being *'salt of the earth'*
is notoriously hard to pin down. Salt had multiple uses. Was Jesus
referring to flavouring, or to keeping something good and useful,
or to fertilising to help things be more fruitful? Rather than worry
about which option to select, perhaps we should assume that, as
with so many of Jesus' analogies, it has multiple useful meanings.
In a small-group setting, we could ask people to consider what it
looks like to be salt and light in a time of transition, and point to
possible answers like:

- being 'out there' to be seen, noticed and beneficial on our
  frontlines – making a positive difference through our presence;
- staying true to Jesus in word and deed, so that we are genuinely
  useful and helpful;
- doing good work (the word for 'deeds' in verse 16 includes
  work, tasks and employment);
- others noticing us and being positively changed as a result,
  even to the point of glorifying God themselves.

We need to remember that times of transition are far from all
good. For example, being made redundant is a very different
moment of transition from getting a new job, but we should
acknowledge this too. Discipleship covers the whole of life
and therefore absolutely includes the difficult and challenging
moments. So, as well as comforting the person and recognising
the embarrassment and shame they may be feeling about losing
their job, we could pray for their example as a person of peace
in times of stress or uncertainty, for God to continue to work
through the example they set, and that he will provide a new job
that is right for them.

Retirement is another very different moment of transition – brilliant for some people, terrifying for others. Again, it is absolutely worth marking, because retirement is full of just as many opportunities for fruitfulness as work or young family life. It's the perfect opportunity to look back with thankfulness, and pray for ongoing impact in the roles the person has held, as well as praying for and commissioning them to new frontlines. Retirement is a pivotal moment and a pivotal test for whole-life discipleship; it can sometimes mark the moment when Christians lose contact with non-Christians and start spending almost all their time in gathered-church activities. Finding new frontlines may take extra effort.

We can't possibly mark every significant moment of transition. But we can be alert to them and create a culture where it's known that these important times in people's lives matter to us as a church, sending a powerful message about the value of these times to God.

Of course, when we acknowledge any new job or role, we are also reinforcing and endorsing our view that all work matters to God, including for those not changing jobs at the moment. We are encouraging our people, who in the week ahead will be filling in the month-end accounts spreadsheet, driving a bus, picking up a sales call, changing a nappy, writing an essay on post-structuralism in French literature for uni, fixing a blocked pipe behind the toilet cistern. They are all reminded to see their work as part of the mission of the church.

This moment of change for one person is therefore an opportunity to say to everyone that we all have work to do, whether paid or unpaid, and each task is an opportunity to join God's work in the world, making earth more like heaven and blessing our fellow creatures. Work matters deeply to God. It's how he achieves what he wants done in the world. Our work has the potential to mirror the character of God, who worked at creation and works still. Our work can release potential, make provision, create beauty, bring order out of chaos and enable human flourishing.

Pray about it

Lord, help us not to miss major moments of transition in your people's lives.

Help us make time to pray for and commission them. When we do so, help us to take the opportunity to endorse the role everyone plays for you, everywhere they go. Amen.

Vital sign 18
Major new projects

In a nutshell

New things in church life have a tendency to take the limelight from existing things. Every time we give energy and resources to a new project and communicate about it in detail, there's a danger that other important things will get less airtime. Of course new initiatives and projects need our time, energy and resources to get off the ground. The challenge is to make sure we don't lose the emphasis on our key values, including our value of equipping people as whole-life disciples.

Most churches and church leaders I know are at full capacity most of the time. It's hard to add anything else to our programmes and diaries. There's an argument to be made that many churches would benefit from doing less in their gathered programme, so they can do what they do better and free their people up to spend more time on their frontlines. But the reality is that this is much easier said than done. If we wait for the quieter day before devoting time to discipleship, we may be waiting more earthly days than we have!

Equally, there are seasons when we should absolutely add something significant to our ministry or to the life of the church. It could be a building project or a new community ministry, such as a foodbank, a second service, a drop-in café, a debt counselling service, a job club or a Messy Church programme. There are always new and good ideas to consider, and much wisdom is needed to discern which good idea is for us for this season. As with major issues or crises (see *Vital sign 19*), what qualifies as a 'significant' initiative in one church might not even be worthy of note in another. But whenever a new project is major for you and your church, the lessons and suggestions in this chapter will be helpful.

Whenever we do approach an initiative like this, it's challenging to keep the old but vital things front and centre at the same time as rallying support for the new thing. How do you fund a new building without unintentionally undermining the message that church is not the building? How do you add a mission or ministry without taking away from the message that everyone's life outside the gathered church is their primary mission field and ministry?

There are some questions we can ask ourselves as church leaders that can help here. The first question might be the hardest, when everyone is excited and keen on this new idea: *Does this new initiative or project come from a sacred–secular-divided mindset?* In other words, does the rationale for doing it come from a perspective that puts a higher value on what we do together as a church than what we do apart? If so, should we be doing it at all?

I write this without wanting to dismiss big new initiatives in any way. We completed three big building projects and started multiple new and exciting ministry initiatives over twenty-four years in the church I led. I'm absolutely convinced these new things can be good, right and needed. After all, if the roof's falling in, you've got to fix it. If your town has a debt epidemic, you have to respond to the need. But at the same time, new projects need to be wisely questioned. Do they align with our whole-life values? We shouldn't take this for granted. And while it is often motivating to commit to the exciting new thing, we need to check it doesn't distract from our existing commitments, including our central commitment to disciplemaking.

Continuing with building projects as an example, we need to be cautious if there's a risk that the project will encourage the church to see mission mostly in terms of the building; that the combined costs of divisions, delays, seemingly endless fundraising and massive leadership commitment will dominate the church too much for too long; and that the church will feel it has 'arrived' because of the beautiful new premises, but has neglected actually being missional and discipling each other well.

If after considering these points we're happy that we should launch the new initiative, the second question we need to ask is more subtle. *Is there anything in this project that could be seen as contrary to our desire to grow whole-life disciples?*

We've prayerfully and carefully discerned and agreed that this is the right next big thing for the church. Now that we're pressing 'go', is there anything that could be misunderstood as conveying the message that our church isn't too bothered about whole-life discipleship after all, or that the key mission is the stuff we do under the gathered-church umbrella?

As with so much of church life, the key here is communication. The aim is to make clear what this project is and what it's for, while not over-promising. We can find words to explain how important this new thing is, while at the same time explaining that it's not all-important. Far from putting people off this, honest balance often encourages more people to support the new initiative.

Sometimes quoting other voices that point to our scattered lives as well as our gathered lives can be just what is needed at these times. For example, the Talking Jesus report is a major piece of research on the state of faith in the UK. While considering people's attitudes to Jesus, it recognises the vital role of each Christian's everyday context: 'The reach of the church is greatest through all the normal everyday relationships of practising Christians . . . Relying on a general draw to the gathered church events is going to be problematic. The best bridge is the individual Christian.'[1]

In recent years, the Lausanne Movement has also written extensively about the vital need for a whole-life emphasis and equipping of all of God's people for all of their contexts:

When God chooses and sends his servants, he sends them to all sorts of places, and only occasionally into a local church setting . . . The future of the Christian movement will depend on how we value, train, and empower the 'lay' membership of our churches; for they are the majority. Before our Lord returns, may it be so.[2]

In my own church in Chichester, when we began our biggest building project it was because we had reached capacity. In fact, we were over capacity in all our main Sunday gatherings and much of our activity during the week. We asked ourselves the first question above, and fully believed we were called and led to commit to the building project. Then, throughout the project, which included building a main worship area for more than 300 people, as well as other rooms and facilities, we stressed how important this was, but also that it was *not* the main thing at all. We emphasised the importance of everyone's everyday contexts alongside giving updates about the building. Indeed, if you're thinking about bricks and mortar that everyone can see, it's the perfect time to mention the less visible building we're all engaged in making: '*You also, like living stones, are being built into a spiritual house to be a holy priesthood, offering spiritual sacrifices acceptable to God through Jesus Christ*' (1 Peter 2:5). We are being built into a house, or temple, of the Spirit. We are not just a building with priests in it. We are all priests, everywhere. We are mobile homes for God, wherever he sends us throughout the week.

When my church's building project was close to completion, we planned an opening celebration. I had the 'brilliant' idea of putting up a sign at the back of the stage that read 'This is not it!' Older, wiser leaders in the church pointed out that if new people found their way into our church building out of curiosity, or because they were genuinely searching for meaning and hope in their life for now and eternity, 'This is not it!' may not be the best choice of message to greet them with. They were right, and we never put the sign up. But we did frequently reiterate a message with that phrase.

We would say, 'This is not it, because it's not about the building; it's about the people. This is not it, because we don't think we're special; we are partners and family with the other Christians and churches in our city. This is not it, because we are still in a messy, now-and-not-yet world, waiting for Christ's return. This is not it, because we are imperfect people who need God to help us become more Christ-like every day. This is not it, because we're not just about what happens in the building; we're committed to all the places we find ourselves in throughout the week, and we seek to serve God there.'

When we did open the building, we invited a guest speaker we knew wouldn't spend too much time effervescing about the building but would point us all upwards to God and outwards to his world. All these things helped our church to commit to the building project without reducing commitment to their role as disciples in the whole of their lives. A good way to sum up all these approaches to new projects is to consider two phrases: 'as well as' and 'as part of'.

As well as setting up Messy Church, let's recognise the many ways our people connect with children and young families on their frontlines and seek to help them show and share Jesus in those settings. *As part of* setting up Messy Church, let's recognise that many of those who might start coming will do so because of our people's frontline friendships with them.

As well as creating a debt counselling service, let's encourage and support any in our church who work with or volunteer for organisations supporting people in debt and personal crisis. *As part of* establishing this centre, let's encourage all our people to prayerfully consider who they connect with on their frontlines who need to know about it.

Finally, when we approach new projects, there's a third big question that is worth prayerfully considering: *What would it take for the next big initiative in our church to be about whole-life discipleship – and what could that even look like?*

There's something about the way new ideas come up, often linked to good news stories of initiatives in the UK or the worldwide church, that makes it more likely they'll be focused on gathered-church activities. Equally, a 'big disciplemaking initiative' may not be as visible or viewed as an equal investment. A new building is an investment in the future of the gathered church and the new opportunities it provides. In the same way, whole-life disciplemaking could be something churches intentionally invest in, believing it could be even more noticeable in the long term.

For one church in Harrogate, this meant joining with other churches in the city to establish a commitment to being and growing whole-life disciples across the entire area. So many of their people shared frontlines with Christians from other churches in schools, colleges, hospitals, offices, workplaces, leisure places and beyond. So they ran a major initiative over several years, prayerfully committing to sectors and areas of work and common frontlines.

There's a lesson for all of us here. Whenever it is possible to partner with like-minded churches that share a commitment to equipping their people for everyday discipleship, this is worth pursuing. Those who previously felt alone as Christians on their frontlines are encouraged and empowered by finding others from partner churches in the same workplace or leisure activity, or even in a different but similar type of work or frontline setting. The ability for individual Christians to share frontline challenges and opportunities, and gain prayer support and encouragement, is significantly increased when whole-life church networks and partnerships are made possible.

The challenge for all of us is, first, to seek to discern God's guidance on any new project. Second, when we do commit to a bold new and needed project, we must not lose sight of our key values, including whole-life discipleship. This need not be an either/or thing – we can continue to grow the existing bold and vital value of whole-life discipleship at the same time and, sometimes, as part of the new initiative.

Pray about it

Lord, give us wisdom and discernment for our big new initiatives. Help us to be able to say a brave 'yes' or a brave 'no'. Help us to find the best way to connect the new thing to our established things, including making whole-life disciples. Show us the 'as part of' and 'as well as' opportunities each new project could bring. Amen.

Vital sign 19
When crises happen

In a nutshell

In church life, frontlines can get sidelined by the headlines. It's all too easy for the big problems to be all-consuming and for whole-life challenges and opportunities to be neglected. But whenever we manage to sustain the whole-life discipleship priority amid the crises or problems, we communicate vital lessons.

Some issues in church life and our national consciousness are so big that they seem to take up most of our time and energy as church leaders. I have no desire to make us feel guilty about this. When these headline problems or crises occur, it's perhaps inevitable that some other aspects of church life get less attention. What church leader hasn't had to rearrange a non-urgent meeting or postpone an activity on their own frontline because an emergency situation has occurred for someone connected with the church? It's right to temporarily drop some things for genuinely urgent and important matters. But what about when we find ourselves in a crisis *season* rather than a crisis *moment*? In times like that, how do we address the headline issue while keeping our frontline priority to the fore?

Let's begin thinking about this by looking at the story of Jesus calming the storm in Luke 8:22–25:

One day Jesus said to his disciples, 'Let us go over to the other side of the lake.' So they got into a boat and set out. As they sailed, he fell asleep. A squall came down on the lake, so that the boat was being swamped, and they were in great danger. The disciples went and woke him, saying, 'Master, Master, we're

*going to drown!' He got up and rebuked the wind and the raging
waters; the storm subsided, and all was calm. 'Where is your
faith?' he asked his disciples.*

Just like the disciples in the boat, we can lose our focus during crisis
seasons. We fix our eyes on the circumstances and not on Jesus. In
this gospel story, we see the disciples receiving some coaching from
Jesus about the nature of focused faith. They wake him in panic
and wonder why he doesn't care about all that they're trying to deal
with. He asks them, 'Where is your faith?' He doesn't say, 'You don't
have faith.' Rather he's saying that now is the time to apply it. Faith
is a deliberate action or choice. When we're facing a crisis, we can
get so focused on it that we lose sight of our purpose and mission.
All we can do is look at the storm. But these are the key moments
when our faith in Jesus develops and grows. Uncomfortable though
they are, these are disciplemaking moments.

What qualifies as a major problem or crisis will vary depending
on the church. In essence, though, I'm referring to issues that
require significant attention from the church leader or leaders.
These issues could be internal and related to an aspect of gathered-
church life, or external and related to a national or international
crisis, like the Covid pandemic. They are normally unforeseen; they
weren't in the programme or our diaries. And normally there's no
easy or quick solution to iron them out. So, for example, an internal
crisis could relate to an ethical issue, financial mismanagement
or lack, a sudden, shock resignation (for any number of reasons)
resulting in the closure of a significant ministry, or an accident or
injury to someone involved in a church activity. An external crisis
could look like the Covid pandemic or the cost-of-living crisis that
followed it. The range of possibilities for this category is very wide.
In turn, this means that while any one crisis feels exceptional, crises
in one form or another can be surprisingly frequent.

At the outset, let's be absolutely clear: this chapter is not an
attempt to reduce our response to external problems or crises. If
we have any sort of leadership responsibility in our churches, these
are the times when we're called to step up, stand up and speak up.

We need to be people of words, deeds and prayer in times of great need or great crisis. The teachings of Jesus compel us to be people of good news in times of bad news.

The history of the local church shows many major examples of this, responding to education needs by setting up schools, to health needs with hospitals and hospices, and to orphans' needs with homes and adoption and fostering programmes. Christians have played vital roles for the better in prison reform, housing reform and the ongoing work to bring slavery to an end. Local churches responding to headline problems have been the starting point for national and international charities serving the poorest and some of those in greatest need in society. The church hosts lunch or breakfast clubs for schoolchildren; provides overnight accommodation and food for people sleeping rough; manages foodbanks feeding those in need; and runs Street Pastor schemes helping people stay safe on nights out. On any one day, the local church continues to make a difference to millions of lives, in our neighbourhoods and across the world.

To face these major problems, we need lamenters, problem-solvers and pray-ers. We need lamenters because we need those who grieve what has been lost and what is not right. We need problem-solvers who naturally respond to a challenge with innovative ideas to make things better and turn around a bad situation for good. And we need pray-ers who call out to God for help and hope in seemingly hopeless situations. As church leaders, each of us is probably better at one of these three elements than the other two, but we each need to do all three to the best of our ability. It's right that we give our best at times when the worst is happening or in danger of happening.

Here's the challenge, though. The leadership time that these headline issues consume, and the profile they get in our meetings and gathered times, can lead us unintentionally back to a sacred–secular-divided mindset. They may deserve plenty of airtime, but at the same time what are we conveying about the importance of the opportunities we each get to respond to need, to speak up for justice, to mitigate against crises in our daily lives? Crisis response can never solely be covered by gathered-church initiatives, although there are of course some things that can be better done by a group than an individual. The point, though, is that our corporate response to crises must not crowd out the call each of us has to push back the darkness on our frontlines.

Equally, we can't just say, 'We'll get through this difficult time and afterwards get back to our priorities, including whole-life discipleship.' This would be a mistake for three reasons. First, many major problems last too long to park 'discipleship' in the pending tray. Getting through some issues might last your whole time as leader in your church, and some headline issues last a lifetime.

Second, today's crisis will all too often be swiftly followed by another, which may feel equally time-consuming. We stuck it out through Covid safety measures and lockdowns, and then five minutes later energy bills shot through the ceiling. Similarly, on an internal front, we might navigate a potentially church-splitting disagreement only to then discover a major ethical issue involving someone in leadership. If we're always waiting for a clearer day, we may be waiting a very long time. Our ducks are never all in a row.

Third, as we saw in the passage from Luke, there are often whole-life discipleship lessons to be learned from the crisis we're in. These issues might not be the things we first think of as church leaders, but they could be vital for our people's growth in the faith.

One of the clearest illustrations of how all this works out in practice came during the Covid pandemic. When the first UK lockdown came into force in March 2020, it qualified as a crisis under any church's definition of the term. Some churches had many people desperately ill and dying from Covid. Some had to navigate misunderstandings and misinformation. We all had to plan the best ways of meeting and caring for our people. We worked on new online skills, and when we were allowed onsite meetings, there was so much to navigate according to the various stages and restrictions at the time. In short, as church leaders we needed to be lamenters, problem-solvers and pray-ers. Looking back, I know I probably didn't get the balance of those three right at the time.

In many ways, the early months of the pandemic provided the perfect example of frontlines getting sidelined by the headline. As well as considering our own gathered-church issues, there were, of course, changes to virtually everyone's frontlines. Reflecting back on that time, how much did I ask people about their frontline changes and challenges, and did I focus on the obvious frontlines – those working in the NHS, for example?

Let's consider just one of the opportunities at that time that could so easily have been missed as we struggled to deal with our own church-programme challenges. In times of uncertainty and stress, people share more, looking for safe people with whom to share their concerns and anxieties. During the lockdowns, many Christians became exactly those safe people. The folk in our churches had unique opportunities to be salt and light in that time of crisis, and we had a unique opportunity to encourage and pray for them. Did we take it?

As we moved back to gathering in person and were gradually able to re-establish other elements in the church programme, the lockdown crisis was replaced by new church leadership challenges. Many people who had served for years in particular ministries 'pre-resigned', letting us know they had been re-thinking a sensible life balance (which was fair enough). Just at the moment when some people were excited to see the old show back up and running, others were questioning which parts of it had passed their sell-by date, and we were finding ourselves with fewer people to lead key activities.

When we found ourselves in the midst of this complicated scenario, with competing and contradicting expectations, it was all too easy to forget the whole-life perspective. Because the reality was that many of these people stepping down from leading were seeing the need to give time and priority to their frontlines. That was a good thing! But it didn't feel like it at the time. When someone resigns from something in gathered-church life, it's hard to keep our first thoughts kind and positive. We might sometimes want to question their motives or blame ourselves for not making our serving opportunities sustainable and compelling. We think of the problems and gaps this change causes us.

These feelings are somewhat inevitable, but people resigning from roles is also inevitable. So, do I err on the side of kindness to myself and others and, crucially, do I ask God if there is a bigger kingdom opportunity opening up for them? Sometimes – in fact, often – God may be asking us to do less in the gathered-church programme, and these resignations may signal that. There is an opportunity amid the difficulty of navigating leadership changes to pray for and commission people to their frontlines, as though they've just volunteered for something rather than resigned from it. Because, in truth, they have.

Finally, even when a church has what appears to be a very internal crisis, there are external whole-life implications. Imagine a church with a major internal disagreement (you may not need to work hard to imagine it!). The way we as church leaders navigate this models something for our people's frontlines – there are lessons about being people who hold to our beliefs while disagreeing well. Our actions in times of crisis may provide lessons for very different crises on people's frontlines.

Just as we saw with the previous chapter, the 'as well as' and 'as part of' exercise is helpful here. We need to have the prayerful insight and determination to say that *as well as* devoting the needed prayer, time and energy to this issue, we will not neglect our resolve to equip and encourage people for their frontlines. And *as part of* considering this crisis, we will deliberately step back from gathered-church issues, and prayerfully, carefully ask how it relates to our people's whole-life discipleship and how we can include these issues in our plans.

Pray about it

Lord, when I seek to meet the challenge in front of me today, help me not to miss the challenge in front of people on their frontlines. In a still-broken world, we know you can turn around bad situations for good. When there are significant problems inside or outside our church, help us to see more with your eyes. Help us to serve you well in these times. Amen.

Vital sign 20
Significant appointments

In a nutshell

When someone is preparing to step up into a leadership role in our church, it's crucial we understand their view of whole-life discipleship. We need to make sure it's always on our radar to check and ensure it's a primary consideration in any leadership hiring or appointment process.

Is our church's commitment to whole-life discipleship embedded in the church leaders, or in the church? If the answer isn't 'both', we're in trouble. If the values of whole-life discipleship aren't owned by the leaders, those vital values will be poorly tended and unlikely to survive. And if they aren't owned across the whole church, they will be poorly rooted and will struggle to grow whenever the leaders change. This is especially true when a leader steps down from a role and a vacancy occurs, whether they're a senior leader, minister or pastor, or a leader of a particular ministry within the church.

Whole-life disciplemaking should never be just one particular leader's specialist subject. It should outlast that person's role in the church, otherwise we as a leadership have failed. Of course, our values don't live in the fabric of the buildings. They live in the people, and especially the next generation of leaders. Whenever there is a change in any significant role, an ongoing emphasis of whole-life discipleship is a vital sign of good church health.

The Bible is full of new-appointment and succession stories, and some are more successful than others. For Moses, Mount Pisgah is a significant marker point. When he comes down from the mountain and views what's to come, much of his focus changes to preparing Joshua and Israel for the day he will no longer be with them.

> *'Go up to the top of Pisgah and look west and north and south*
> *and east. Look at the land with your own eyes, since you are*
> *not going to cross this Jordan. But commission Joshua, and*
> *encourage and strengthen him, for he will lead this people*
> *across and will cause them to inherit the land that you will see.'*
> (Deuteronomy 3:27–28)

We have to be very careful when applying Moses' unique story of succession planning to our own leadership roles. Moses had a particular role, and God spoke to him with particular clarity. Often it is healthy and necessary for new leaders to bring fresh perspective rather than repeat our old ways. For me, it is not so much about prescribing a way forward, complete with programme details, but about pointing forward to what we believe are God-given priorities. I'm convinced that whole-life discipleship is one of those priorities that should continue to grow and develop with each new appointment.

Recently, I watched a young leader take a service in a large east London church consisting almost entirely of people from an African heritage background. The event was encouraging and full of life, but what struck me most, having spoken previously to the senior pastor, was the extent to which this young leader so clearly owned the same values, ethos and priorities. In my role for LICC, and my previous role as President of the Baptist Union of Great Britain, I've had the privilege of visiting hundreds of churches across the UK, so the fact that I even noticed this quality on this occasion shows that it isn't always present. It was interesting, therefore, to hear him introduce himself later in the service as 'a child of this church'; he'd been a member of this community since his birth.

If our church has been committed to whole-life discipleship for a good while, then we may have greater confidence that a prospective leader who's been part of the church community for a long time will have caught the values of whole-life discipleship. Experience also shows that when people come to faith and grow as Christians in a church that exhibits these vital signs of whole-life discipleship, they're more likely to naturally 'get it'. After all, how can there be any kind of Christianity other than one that impacts all we say and do? This is especially true for young people and young adults. The generations now assuming leadership for the first time place a high value on consistency and integrity, being truly the same person throughout all aspects of their lives. Whole-life discipleship resonates deeply with this perspective. This is not to say we shouldn't check prospective leaders' understanding of and passion for the vision before they step up to a key role. But there are times when we can confidently pass on the baton.

In truth, the greatest challenges often come when welcoming capable people to our church from another community. Make no mistake, these people can of course be a significant blessing and answer to prayer. Fresh eyes and new perspectives are always healthy, and cross-pollination keeps us growing as a wider church. But even communities that seem very similar on the surface can carry a wide variety of views on a wide variety of things. If we're seeking to embed or nurture a whole-life disciplemaking culture, it's very possible that incoming leaders will join us with a deeply sacred–secular-divided mindset, which risks real damage to what we're trying to achieve.

In the UK today many, or indeed most, Christians don't fully understand the differences we're emphasising here in talking about *whole-life* discipleship. This doesn't mean they aren't wise, kind, willing, servant-hearted people who will step up and serve. But it may mean they are operating automatically from a culture that instinctively prioritises and lionises gathered-church activities and has little to say to or about everyday ministry. The fact that they're starting from this point of sacred–secular-divided thinking when they come to our church or apply for the role doesn't preclude them from embracing the whole-life emphasis our church is working on. But it's wise to check they have genuinely moved from 'not getting it' to 'embracing it' before putting them in a position that helps set the culture.

Part of ensuring newcomers quickly latch on to whole-life discipleship is to make the concept part of the welcome to everyone who joins the church. Whether we 'induct' newcomers through a course, a talk or an informal dinner, we need to make sure we set out our best argument for the importance of whole-life discipleship. For example, one church in the Midlands offers a regular introductory course for new people. As part of the course, they invite people to bring an item that represents their frontline – a stethoscope for a doctor, a trowel for the retired person with an allotment, a tennis racquet for the person who's part of the tennis club, and so on. They then use these items as prompts to pray for and commission people back to their frontlines, explaining and embodying the church's care for ministry in all of life.

In my church leadership, I sought to ensure our welcome to new people included an overview like the following:

A key value for us in this church is what happens outside of the church building – in your everyday life, wherever that is, Monday to Saturday as well as Sunday. Put simply, we believe it all matters to God. Your everyday matters matter. Whether they feel spiritual or not, they have spiritual significance, because God is at work through the Holy Spirit in every part of his creation. And in all your tasks, places and relationships, you get to join in with his redemption plan. In this place, we are about every other place – the places you go to from here. Workplaces, homes, leisure places, neighbourhoods and beyond. What happens when we gather together really matters. God is with us here and we treasure that. And God is in those other places too. As a church, we believe we will never do what God has called us to do until we make every effort to equip people for every place they go.

Even with a thorough 'welcome pipeline' like this, though, it can still be tricky to make sure a potential new leader truly understands and cares about the vision. Whole-life discipleship is simple but subtle.

For example, one common near-but-not-quite understanding is to equate whole-life discipleship with the church's work in the 'community'. When it comes to thinking about whole-life discipleship we need to be a little cautious with this word. 'Community' has become something of a catch-all term that can mean a wide variety of things to different people. When some talk of work 'in the community', often they still mean the things that happen within the church programme but perhaps not on church premises. And in this case the people who make up 'the community' are often not people we naturally rub shoulders with for the majority of our time. 'The community' can sometimes refer to faces we serve rather than friends we spend time with. Crucially, in this use of the term we're often still referring to voluntary time Christians give to church activities. This type of church work is, of course, good, valuable and to be celebrated. But if we stop there, slipping into the belief that 'blessing the community' means running church-led ministries, we've still not genuinely explored whole-life discipleship for the majority of our people.

In fact, it's possible to employ a lot of the words we've used in this book – ideas like 'frontlines' and 'everyday mission' – and still fail to truly convey the full wonder of the gospel for all of life; still fail to truly nurture a culture that cares just as much about people's ordinary places as their time in church. So how might we assess whether prospective leaders have genuinely taken the whole-life vision to heart, without forcing every willing person through some kind of entrance exam?

One way is to ask about their previous church. For example, did it share this same emphasis on whole-life discipleship? If so, can they describe what that meant, or what it looked like? If their previous church didn't focus on whole-life disciplemaking, can they name the differences they've noticed in your church? If they don't see or can't name any differences, that could be a concern.

With all this said, the reality is that this is an extremely challenging thing to get right. All too frequently we have all too few gifted and willing volunteers stepping up to serve in the church and it can be very difficult to make the right appointments.

There is huge pressure to fill the gaps and keep the show on the road. But getting it right really does matter, because in all leadership roles, the post-holder's words and values leak out into the wider church culture. New appointments will either support or undermine our desire to encourage and equip people for all of their lives. If we don't appoint people with whole-life discipleship as a central consideration of their role, it's possible for a church that's genuinely seeking to work at all the vital signs in this book to end up with:

- a preacher who mentions how unimportant their work is, and that their role in church is what they live for;
- a children's or youth worker whose ultimate success story would be if one or two of their group grew up to fulfil paid ministry roles in the church;
- a small group leader who doesn't connect the Bible study with their members' everyday lives;
- a worship leader who introduces the time of sung worship by inviting people to forget about the week they have just had and concentrate on Jesus;
- a leader of the retirees' group who thinks whole-life discipleship only applies to paid work and isn't so relevant for their age bracket;
- a keen person with a vision to create a new ministry that might be very popular, but is also very likely to consume even more of people's time in fellowship with one another at the expense of time on their frontlines.

Getting new appointments right and planning succession is always challenging. The example of Moses and Joshua reminds us that God is in charge of these appointments rather than us. He invites us as church leaders to seek his guidance. When vital God-given values – including whole-life discipleship – flourish but also find fresh expression after a new appointment, we have a winning combination.

Pray about it

Lord, thank you for every person willing to step up and serve. Help us to get the balance right between vital and helpful roles in the gathered church and vital and helpful roles for your people in the scattered church. Help us to help your people understand and embrace the need to be whole-life disciples and to communicate and convey this wherever they serve in our church. Amen.

CONCLUSION

If this is the end, where do we start?

I really hope you've enjoyed this book. I also hope that by now we can agree on just how important it is for our churches to be inspired to encourage and equip Christians in their everyday lives.

The sum total of twenty chapters' worth of tips and suggestions could be daunting, so where should you start? To help you answer that question, below are four ways to find the right whole-life disciplemaking moves for the season ahead in your particular context.

Whatever you choose to do next, it's important to acknowledge that every step in the right direction is worth making, however big or small. Don't feel pressured to do everything. Take joy in the small victories, and ask God to work through your efforts to inspire your people for the roles he's given them out in the world.

1 Use the *Vital Signs Assessment Tool*

If you've not yet used the free *Vital Signs Assessment Tool* (see page 11), take 15 minutes to answer the multiple choice questions and get your tailored report, either on your own or, better yet, as a whole leadership team. It'll point you to key areas where you can begin to make progress. Find it at **licc.org.uk/vitalsigns** or scan the QR code below.

2 Pray through the four key areas in this book

The twenty vital signs are grouped into four sections: your individual ministry, the time when we're gathered together, time spent planning, and when opportunities arise and we need to respond. Take some time to consider each of the four areas of church life we've discussed, ideally with the other members of your team. Think through each area in turn and prayerfully ask if, in each one, there is a next move starting point for you and your church to embed whole-life discipleship there. Again, the *Vital Signs Assessment Tool* will help you here.

3 Examine your church calendar

Another way to consider the twenty chapters is in terms of the church calendar or seasons of church life. Some of the chapters typically refer to daily things, some are weekly, others are monthly or termly, some are annual, and some may be very occasional – less frequent than yearly. The exact level of frequency of some of the chapters will vary greatly in different churches, but you should be able to identify the typical frequency of each in your church. Below is a starting-point example:

Daily
Daily prayer
Daily Bible reading
Pastoral care
Leading by example
Daily conversations

Weekly
Sunday gatherings
Age- and stage-focused work
Prayer meetings and small groups

Communications
When the frontline comes to us

Monthly/termly
Leaders' meetings
Programme planning
Births, deaths, marriages and baptisms

Yearly
Annual festivals and seasons
AGMs and annual reviews
Annual opportunities

Occasionally
When crises happen
Significant appointments
Major new projects
Times of transition

This example will almost certainly not be a perfect fit for your church. For example, the chapter 'Births, deaths, marriages and baptisms' might apply weekly for some churches, while for others these may be a less than yearly occurrence. Adjust the headings to fit your context. Like the example above, you don't have to have an equal number of vital signs under each heading and timescale.

Once you have formed your own calendar, you can ask two questions:

- Do we have a really strong example of whole-life discipleship in each timescale (daily, weekly, monthly/termly, yearly and occasionally), which we can celebrate and seek to further embed?
- Is there a clear area we think we're currently weak on in each timescale (daily, weekly, monthly/termly, yearly and occasionally)?

Answers to both of these questions should provide good next-step starting points for making real progress.

4 Identify areas of strength and weakness

For a quick start, you can simply name the two or three vital signs you believe are strongest and weakest in your church and discuss them with the other leaders in your team. The *Vital Signs Assessment Tool* will identify these clearly for you. Great progress can be made by giving thanks for, valuing and working at areas of strength, as well as by identifying, praying into and working to improve areas of relative weakness.

* * *

These vital signs should never be a one-hit wonder. The greatest value will be in identifying vital signs to focus on, for now, using any of the suggestions above and then naming a time, six months or a year ahead, to review – perhaps at an annual leaders' away day. The *Vital Signs Assessment Tool* is designed for this. Later tests can be compared with previous ones for your church to identify areas where progress has been, or still needs to be, made.

The aim, always, is not to be daunted by the number of areas to consider but to be encouraged that genuine progress is doable for all of us and each step forward is worth making. The level of change a church can achieve by identifying two or three key areas for the year ahead should not be underestimated.

Wherever you start, begin with prayer, including the prayers at the end of each chapter. Every bit of discipleship progress worth celebrating starts and ends with prayer.

My hope and prayer is that our Lord would point you to your key vital signs for the vital work of disciplemaking in your church, for the season you're in and whatever lies ahead. And may he do that for each of us.

Notes

Introduction

1 Mark Greene, *Imagine How We Can Reach the UK* (Milton Keynes: Authentic Lifestyle, 2004), p. 24.

2 While John Stott referred to 'double listening', his practice and teaching had these triple-listening aspects, as we point out here. See: https://licc.org.uk/resources/wise-peacemakers-part-1-of-5/ (accessed 30 November 2023). See also John Stott, *The Contemporary Christian* (London: IVP, 1992), 101–113, with its three-fold structure of listening to God, to one another and to the world.

Vital sign 1

1 Edwin and Lillian Harvey, *The Christian's Daily Challenge* (Berea, KY: Harvey Christian Publishers Inc., 2018).

2 John Wesley's teaching on prayer is famously quoted this way. It is difficult to be certain whether this is a direct quotation or a simplified summary.

Vital sign 2

1 'Sustaining Change' report, available at: https://licc.org.uk/app/uploads/2021/06/LICC-Sustaining-Change-Report-2021 (accessed 1 December 2023), page 9.

Vital sign 3

1 'Sustaining Change' report, available at: https://licc.org.uk/app/uploads/2021/06/LICC-Sustaining-Change-Report-2021 (accessed 1 December 2023).

2 Richard J. Foster, *Prayers from the Heart* (San Francisco, CA: HarperOne, 1994), p. xi.

3 Quoted in Richard J. Foster, *Streams of Living Water: Celebrating the great traditions of Christian Faith* (Fount, 1999), p. 237.

Vital sign 4

1 Neil Hudson, *Imagine Church: Releasing dynamic everyday disciples* (London: IVP, 2012), pp. 116–17.
2 'Sustaining Change' report, pp. 51–54, available at: https://licc.org. uk/app/uploads/2021/06/LICC-Sustaining-Change-Report-2021 (accessed 1 December 2023).

Vital sign 5

1 'Sustaining Change' report, p. 51, available at: https://licc.org.uk/app/ uploads/2021/06/LICC-Sustaining-Change-Report-2021 (accessed 1 December 2023).
2 'Sustaining Change' report, p. 52.
3 Frederick Buechner, *Now and Then* (San Francisco: Harper & Row, 1983), available at: https://www.frederickbuechner.com/quote-of-the-day/2017/1/1/life-itself-is-grace (accessed 12 December 2023).
4 See, for example, J. Huckins and R. Yackley, *Thin Places: Six postures for creating and practicing missional community* (The House Studio, 2012). The Celtic monk St Columba described a thin place as 'a location where heaven and earth seemed only thinly separated'.
5 'Sustaining Change' report, p. 52.

Vital sign 6

1 It seems Wesley met 'a serious man' who said this to him first and it subsequently became part of Wesley's teaching (John Telford, *The Life of John Wesley*, 1906).

Vital sign 7

1 LICC, 'Making Disciples for Everyday Life', see: https://licc.org. uk/ourresources/making-disciples-for-everyday-life/ (accessed 12 December 2023).

Vital sign 8

1 Available at: https://www.barna.com/research/

six-reasons-young-christians-leave-church/ (accessed 12 December 2023).

Vital sign 12

1 Malcolm Gladwell, *Blink: The power of thinking without thinking* (London: Penguin, 2005), p. 114.

Vital sign 13

1 Kierkegaard's original words on this theme were longer and written and published in a Danish journal in 1843. It is most often translated to the shortened version quoted here.

Vital sign 17

1 From 'Archbishop Justin Welby in conversation with Nicky Gumbel' available on YouTube https://youtu.be/fjwmRnfwTbU?si=BksowP6B1YYcWt5f – starting at 13 min 26 seconds (accessed 25 January 2024).

2 This prayer is adapted from a prayer from the Church of England's online 'Prayers for life events', available at: https://www.churchofengland.org/prayer-and-worship/topical-prayers/prayers-life-events (accessed 25 January 2024).

Vital sign 18

1 'Talking Jesus Report 2022', available at: https://talkingjesus.org/research (accessed 8 December 2023).

2 Available at: https://lausanne.org/about/blog/the-measure-of-a-servant (accessed 8 December 2023).

About LICC

Imagine if every Christian lived their life as Jesus would. . .

It would transform the people and places around them. It would change their organisations, communities and societies. And it would change the world – as God works in and through them, right where they are.

But most Christians tell us they have neither the vision nor the tools for the task. That's where LICC comes in. We were established by John Stott in 1982 to help Christians integrate the gospel in all of life and see it impact the wider world. We're here to empower Christians to relate the good news of Jesus to all of life. And we work to help people know God more deeply, bringing his wisdom, grace and truth to everything they do, wherever they are – at work, at college and at home; in the pub, the shops and the gym; on social media, in the office and out with friends.

We call this 'whole-life discipleship'. It looks like bearing fruit in every sphere of life: making good work, modelling godly character, ministering grace and love, moulding culture, and being a mouth-piece for truth and justice and a messenger of the gospel. It's about being fully alive.

To make it happen, we work with individuals, church leaders and those who train them, partnering with organisations across denominations and networks. We delve into the Bible, think hard about contemporary culture, and listen carefully to God's people, exploring the challenges and opportunities they face. What we do comes out of what we learn. Creative communications, resources, events, training, articles, books, films, stories and more – all designed to support whole-life discipleship.

Jesus calls people into a movement of hope that will bring life to every human being and the entire planet. Today, the need for whole-life disciples is as great as ever. We're working to engage over a million Christians with this whole-life vision.

What does fruitfulness
look like in our everyday lives?

Mark Greene

FRUITFULNESS
ON THE FRONTLINE.

Making a difference
where you are

Available Now

9781783591251 | Paperback | 208 Pages

 books

How can an ordinary church grow disciples who live their whole lives as followers of Jesus?

Neil Hudson

Imagine
Church

Releasing Whole
Life Disciples

Available Now

9781844745661 | Paperback | 192 Pages

ivp books

A study series on seven books of the Bible, covering seven genres, with a whole-life discipleship focus.

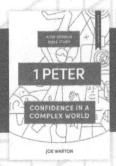

9781789740868
Paperback | 72 pp

9781789740820
Paperback | 72 pp

9781789740844
Paperback | 80 pp

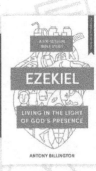

9781789741612
Paperback | 80 pp

9781789741629
Paperback | 80 pp

9781789742787
Paperback | 80 pp

9781789743661
Paperback | 80 pp

Available Now

ivp books